INSIGHT POCKET GUIDES

BOSTON

Discover America

GW00362529

APA PUBLICATIONS

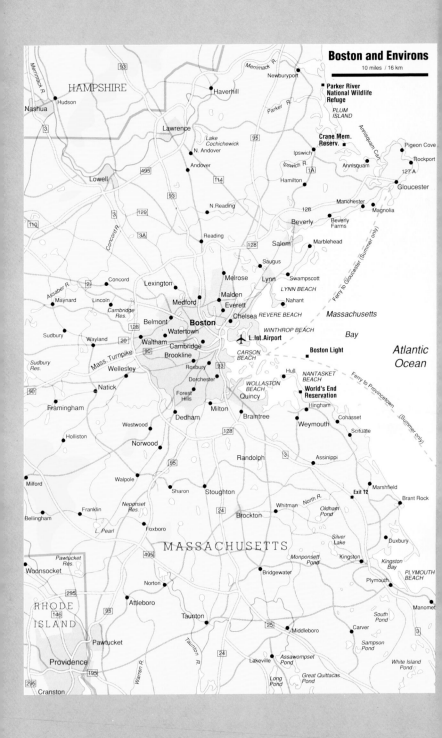

Boston and Environs

10 miles / 16 km

NEW HAMPSHIRE

Merrimack R.
Newburyport

Parker River
National Wildlife
Refuge

PLUM
ISLAND

Nashua
Hudson
Haverhill
Parker R.

Lawrence
Lake
Cochichewick
N. Andover

Crane Mem.
Reserv.

Pigeon Cove
Rockport

Ipswich
Ipswich R.
Annisquam

Annisquam Can.

Ferry to Gloucester (Summer only)

127 A

Andover
114
Hamilton
1A

Lowell
495
Gloucester

93
N. Reading
128
Manchester
Magnolia

3
129
Reading
Beverly
Beverly
Farms

110
Concord R.
3A
128
Salem
Marblehead

Assaber R.
Concord
Lexington
Melrose
Saugus
Swampscott

2
Maynard
Lincoln
Medford
Malden
Lynn
LYNN BEACH

Cambridge
Res.
Belmont
Everett
Nahant

Sudbury
Wayland
Watertown
Chelsea
REVERE BEACH

128
Waltham
Cambridge
WINTHROP BEACH

20
90
Brookline
L. Int. Airport

Sudbury
Res.
Wellesley
Roxbury
CARSON
BEACH
Boston Light

Natick
93
Dorchester
Hull
NANTASKET
BEACH

Framingham
Forest
Hills
WOLLASTON
BEACH
Quincy
World's End
Reservation

Holliston
Westwood
Milton
Braintree
Hingham
Cohasset

Norwood
128
Weymouth
Scituate

Milford
95
Randolph
3
Assinippi

Walpole
Sharon
Stoughton
Marshfield
Exit 12
Brant Rock

Franklin
Neponset
Res.
Whitman
North R.
Oldham
Pond

Bellingham
L. Pearl
Foxboro
Brockton
24

MASSACHUSETTS
Silver
Lake
Duxbury

495
Monponsett
Pond
Kingston
Kingston
Bay
PLYMOUTH
BEACH

Pawtucket
Res.
Norton
Bridgewater
Plymouth

Woonsocket
295
25
Middleboro
Carver
South
Pond
Manomet

RHODE
ISLAND
146
95
Attleboro
Taunton
24
Lakeville
Assawompset
Pond
Sampson
Pond
3

Pawtucket
Taunton R.
Warren R.
Long
Pond
Great Quittacas
Pond
White Island
Pond

Providence
195

295
Cranston

Massachusetts
Bay

Atlantic
Ocean

Ferry to Provincetown   (Summer only)

Dear Visitor!

Boston is not only the most historic city in America, but also one of the most livable: small enough so that walking is not a lost art, large enough to provide the diversity that makes urban life interesting. And despite its host of monuments, it is also a young city, on account of the hundreds of thousands of students at the 50 colleges and universities.

In these pages *Insight Guides'* correspondent in Boston, Marcus Brooke, has devised a range of itineraries to bring you the best of Boston. Three full-day tours cover Boston and Cambridge: from the Freedom Trail and the Public Garden to a tour of Harvard University. Six additional half-day outings can be taken either in the morning, afternoon or evening. But *Insight Pocket Guide: Boston* doesn't stop there. It goes on to a full-day excursion to Concord and Lexington, followed by a wealth of ideas on shopping, eating out, nightlife and where to stay.

 Marcus Brooke was first lured to Boston by its bastions of education, particularly Harvard Medical School. As a faculty member at Harvard and, later, Massachusetts Institute of Technology, he enjoyed the best of two worlds – Boston and Cambridge. He has now been on the road with Insight Guides for over 20 years and is the editor of *Insight Guide: Boston*. It gives him great pleasure, he says, to share with you the history, landscape and architecture of this rich, fascinating area, a place where, in the words of Charles Mackay, 'the onus lies upon every respectable person to prove he has not written a sonnet, preached a sermon, or delivered a lecture.'

Hans Höfer
Publisher, Insight Guides

C O N T E N T S

Pages 2/3:
Rowe's wharf

*Pages 8/9:
Boston blooms
in spring*

HISTORY

'**W**e must consider that we shall be a City upon a Hill. The eyes of all people are upon us.' Thus John Winthrop exhorted his fellow Puritans aboard the *Arbella* which, in 1630, was en route from England to the New World. On reaching the New World the Puritans first landed at Salem, 20 miles north of Boston, but, finding the town in a 'sad and unexpected condition,' they soon moved south to Charlestown. Here, foul drinking water felled the settlers at an alarming rate. When they were visited by the Reverend William Blackstone, who invited them to his home on what is now Boston's Beacon Hill (but was then called Shawmut), they not only accepted but, like *The Man Who Came to Dinner*, they remained.

Early settlers

Blackstone, who had arrived with a gang of adventurers from England some years before, was squeezed out, and because of its hilly topography the Puritans changed Shawmut's name to Trimountain. Had Winthrop foresight in saying, 'we shall be a City upon a Hill,' or had he consulted with Captain John Smith who, in 1614, had made a detailed survey of the Massachusetts Bay region?

Soon after, in honor of that town in Lincolnshire, England, from where many of the settlers had come, Trimountain became Boston. Much later the hills were truncated. Their soil was used to fill the marshes that surrounded the original Shawmut, and in this man-

Culture

ner first the South End and then the Back Bay were created.

The settlement, whose charter from James I designated it the Massachusetts Bay Company, enjoyed virtual autonomy from the mother country for almost 50 years. It developed as a society in which religion and government were inseparable. A moral code was strictly enforced, and education was of paramount importance. Six years after their arrival, the Puritans established Harvard, across the river from Boston in Cambridge, as a college for ministers.

Boston prospered, with its wealth coming from the sea in the shape of cod fishing, whaling, ship building and a maritime trade made possible by the excellent natural harbor. Soon – and until 1755, when Philadelphia won the honor – its population was the largest in North America, and by the year 1700 it boasted the third largest fleet in the British realm.

The calm was disturbed in 1684, however, when London, irritated because Boston's economic success was making inroads into its

The Long Wharf and harbor as painted by Byron in 1764

The Boston Massacre, 1770

profits, abrogated the Massachusetts Bay charter. Two years later, Sir Edmund Andros was installed as the first royal governor of the Province of Massachusetts Bay. Andros ruled like a despot, creating new taxes and granting lands to his favorites. When word of the overthrow of James II reached Boston, it took but a jiffy to imprison him.

During the next century, England continued to impose increasingly damaging taxes on the young Boston economy. 'Taxation without representation is tyranny' became a rallying cry in Boston and resulted in the arrival of two regular regiments of British troops in 1768. Confrontation, even on a small scale, was inevitable, and 1770 saw the Boston Massacre, in which five men were killed by British soldiers after a petty fracas. This occurred on the very day when all taxes, except for a nominal Tea Tax, were revoked.

Hatred continued unabated, and three years later nearly 100 patriots dressed as Indians attended the Boston Tea Party and hurled 340 crates of tea into the harbor. King George ordered the closure of the the port and sent more troops to Boston. Meanwhile, throughout New England, militia units drilled and built up arms caches: further confrontation was inevitable.

The American Revolution began in and around Boston, and the great moments in that war – Paul Revere's midnight ride, 'the shot heard 'round the world' and the Battle of Bunker Hill – are inscribed on the pages of history. When George Washington, who had assumed command of the Continental Army in July 1775, fortified Dorchester Heights in a single night, the bell at last tolled

The Battle of Bunker Hill

for the British, who realized that their position was untenable. They evacuated on March 17, 1776, and peace, accompanied by an economic depression because of the sudden loss of the British markets, resulted.

After the Revolution

With Yankee ingenuity the city's merchants set out to find new goods for new markets. In 1790 the *Columbia*, a Boston vessel, returned after a three-year circumnavigation of the world, and the following year 70 Yankee merchantmen sailed from Boston for China, Europe and the Indies. Boston attained greater prosperity than ever before. A census at this time revealed the population to be 18,320 – a figure which increased nearly 15-fold over the next 100 years.

The War of 1812 resulted in a temporary setback, paralyzing the city's commerce and causing the decline of its maritime supremacy. Manufacturing and industry took up the slack. Textile mills were opened in the 1810s, and the mid-1830s saw the appearance of the nation's railroads, largely funded with Boston money. Shipping had one last romantic gasp in the 1840s and early 1850s when glorious clippers such as the *Flying Cloud* were built, but after this the harbor fell into disuse. It has enjoyed a revival only as recently as the 1950s and 1960s, its success in large part due to leisure pursuits.

George Washington

Liberal Boston shone in the 1830s, when William Lloyd Garrison and others thundered forth on the abolition of the slave trade. How they would have suffered if they had witnessed the dreadful blotting of the city's history book with its negative reaction to busing (the transporting of black children to better schools in white neighborhoods) in 1974.

The 19th century was also the period of the Brahmins, a term coined by Oliver Wendell Holmes to describe aristocratic individuals, some of whom claimed to trace their ancestry to the *Arbella*, 'with their houses by Bulfinch, their monopoly of Beacon Street, their ancestral portraits and Chinese porcelain, humanitarianism, Unitarian faith in the march of mind, Yankee shrewdness and New England exclusiveness.'

A Center of Education

This was the century, especially the second half, when Boston earned its renown as the most diversified and dynamic center of education, culture and medical-scientific activities in the United States. Oliver

THE MAYOR OF THE POOR

BOSTON CITY HOSPITAL

Humane Experienced Leadership
ELECT
CURLEY

The people's hero

Wendell Holmes, a Brahmin through and through, summed it up succinctly: 'All I claim for Boston is that it is the thinking center of the continent, and therefore of the planet.'

How the founding Puritans, whose principal concerns included education, would purr if they could see the large numbers of young students strolling on Newbury Street today. Boston, it has been said, 'beds down more students per square civic inch than any other metropolis in the world.' And the reason that students from throughout the world flock to the half-hundred institutes of higher education in Greater Boston is that many are *numero uno* in their own league. Already in 1796 the president of Yale, on a visit to Boston, had remarked: 'Knowledge is probably more universally diffused here than in any other considerable town in the world.'

Harvard, Massachusetts Institute of Technology (MIT) and predominantly single-sex Wellesley have earned a worldwide reputation, but many might not be aware that Boston College is possibly the best Catholic school in the nation and that Brandeis occupies a

Workers on the wharves

George Bush and François Mitterand attend graduation at Boston University

similar position among Jewish schools. Boston University is said to be the best city school in America, and Northeastern University is the largest private school in the nation. Berklee College of Music bows the knee to none in the field of contemporary music, while Emerson is the only four-year college in the land totally oriented to the communication arts and sciences.

Interspersed among the campuses of these famous schools are some of Boston's great cultural institutes – the Public Library, Symphony Hall, the Museum of Fine Arts – all founded in the late nineteenth century.

A Melting Pot

This was also the century when, in the 1840s, a spreading rot took hold of the Irish potato crop and the Irish poured into Boston. By 1855, some 55,000 had settled, mainly in the North End, and soon they, as subsequently demonstrated by James Curley, John F Fitzgerald (the legendary 'Honey Fitz'), and the Kennedy clan, were busy climbing the political ladder and conducting their careers in a from-the-hip style. Irish-born Hugh O'Brien was elected mayor in 1885, starting a Hibernian tradition that still predominates. Indeed, until recently,'Irish only need apply' could well have

been the sign above the mayor's office. The Boston Irish – has any other city given its name to the Irish? – are one big extended family. As a result Boston is, of course, quite free of corruption for 'What is wrong with a father helping a son?' The last few years have seen a new wave of thousands of illegal Irish immigrants who find jobs as construction workers, barmaids and mothers' helpers; the Irish tricolor even flies outside homes in South Boston.

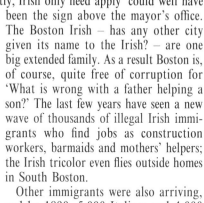

Other immigrants were also arriving, and by 1890, 5,000 Italians and 4,000 Jews lived in Boston, figures which by 1910 had become respectively 30,000 and 40,000. Thirty years later, in the 1940s, blacks from the South relocated in Boston and over the next 30 years the black population increased seven-fold. Then, almost a century after the first tidal wave of Jewish immigrants, Boston was bolstered by a wave of Russian Jews, followed by Asians (especially Vietnamese),

15

Hispanics, especially from El Salvador, and Haitians. The face of the city was changed forever.

By 1990, as a result of people leaving the inner city for the suburbs, the population had fallen to about 580,000 from its 1950 peak of 800,000. Of these, 25 percent are African American, 10 percent Hispanic and 5 percent Asian.

The Twentieth Century

The first half of the 20th century was not an especially dynamic period for Boston. However, after World War II, although the city's Brahmins continued to converse with each other they also widened their circle of acquaintances to include the Irish. Both

groups discovered that they could work together, and in 1957 a renaissance began with the launching of the Boston Redevelopment Authority, which over the next 15 years would carry out urban renewal projects covering 11 percent of the city's land. This exceeded those in any city of comparable size though at the cost of destroying entire neighborhoods. The 1960s were a time of turmoil in Boston. It was not until the 1970s that a real renaissance – spurred in part by the exemplary revitalization of Faneuil Hall Marketplace – began to transform the city.

The following years saw a new industrial revolution. Route 128, a highway encircling the city, is lined with so many high-tech firms that it is known as America's Technol-

Red Sox fans

ogy Highway. By the 1980s, Boston was the hub of the Massachusetts Miracle, based largely on high tech and venture capital. Even the recession that afflicted all New England in the 1990s has done little to dim Boston's spirits.

Boston Today

It would be difficult to over-emphasize the importance of the Catholic church in Boston but there is in fact a purely local religion which binds the population together. It is called Red Sox, the city's baseball team. Come summer and if the Sox are on a roll, then all is well and all Boston walks tall. Let the September Swoon come – as it almost invariably does – and life is scarcely worth living. Recently, a rabbi in his Yom Kippur (Day of Atonement) sermon suggested that his congregation would know when the Messiah had arrived, for only then would the Red Sox win the World Series.

Historical Highlights

1625 William Blackstone, Boston's first colonist, settles on the Common.

1630 Puritan English under John Winthrop form Massachusetts Bay Company colony at Charlestown.

1635 Boston Latin School, the first public school in the nation, is founded.

1636 Harvard College founded.

1684 Crown transforms virtually independent Massachusetts Bay Company into a royal colony whose governor will be appointed by the king.

1690 The first American newspaper *Publick Occurrences: Both Foreign and Domestic* is published in Boston.

1716 Boston Light, the oldest lighthouse in the nation, is erected in the harbor.

1770 Boston Massacre.

1773 Boston Tea Party.

1775 Paul Revere's ride and Battles of Lexington and Concord.

1775 Battle of Bunker Hill and burning of Charlestown.

1775 War of Independence.

1775 George Washington assumes command of Continental Army at Cambridge.

1776 British troops leave Province of Massachusetts.

1776 Declaration of Independence announced from State House.

1789 Constitution framed and John Hancock declared first governor of state of Massachusetts.

1798 Bulfinch's State House graces the city.

1812 War of 1812 paralyzes city's commerce and marks decline of Boston's maritime supremacy.

1821 English High School, the first high school in the nation, is opened.

1822 Boston is incorporated as a city.

1841 The first Irish immigrants arrive as a result of the potato famine in Ireland.

1852 The Boston Public Library opens; it is the first free city library supported by taxes.

1861 Massachusetts Institute of Technology granted charter.

1872 Great Fire of Boston sweeps 65 acres of downtown.

1874 The first words are spoken over the telephone by Alexander Graham Bell.

1877 Swan boats launched at the Public Garden.

1879 Founding of Radcliffe College, sister to Harvard.

1879 Mary Baker Eddy founds Christian Science Church.

1881 Boston Symphony Orchestra is founded.

1897 First Boston marathon.

1897 The first subway in the nation opens in Boston.

1903 Boston is the site of first World Series – Red Sox win.

1910 Dam built to form Charles River Basin.

1946 John F Kennedy elected Congressman for Charlestown and Cambridge.

1948 Polaroid Land Camera invented in Cambridge.

1954 Enders, Robbins, Weller win Nobel prize for work which leads to poliomyelitis vaccine.

1954 Beginning of New England high-tech revolution centered on Greater Boston.

1957 The Boston Redevelopment Authority is launched by Mayor John Hynes.

1980s 'Massachusetts Miracle' high-tech revolution results in economic boom.

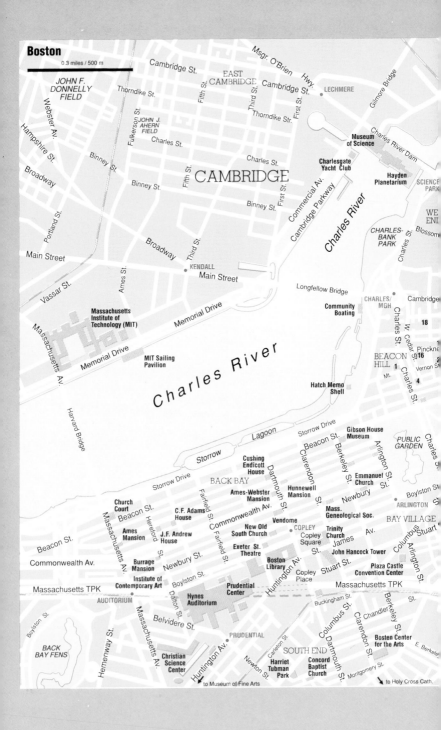

Boston

0.3 miles / 500 m

JOHN F. DONNELLY FIELD

Cambridge St.

Thorndike St.

EAST CAMBRIDGE

Cambridge St.

Msgr. O'Brien Hwy.

LECHMERE

Gilmore Bridge

Webster Av.

Hampshire St.

Fulkerson St.

JOHN J. AHERN FIELD

Charles St.

Fifth St.

Third St.

Thorndike Str.

Museum of Science

Charles River Dam

Broadway

Binney St.

Fifth St.

Charles St.

CAMBRIDGE

Charlesgate Yacht Club

Hayden Planetarium

SCIENCE PARK

Binney St.

Binney St.

First St.

Commercial Av.

Cambridge Parkway

Charles River

WE ENI

Blossom

CHARLES-BANK PARK

Charles

Main Street

Portland St.

Broadway

Third St.

KENDALL

Main Street

Charles River

Vassar St.

Ames St.

Longfellow Bridge

Community Boating

CHARLES/MGH

Cambridge

Massachusetts Institute of Technology (MIT)

Memorial Drive

W. Cedar St.

Charles St.

18

Massachusetts Av.

Memorial Drive

MIT Sailing Pavilion

BEACON HILL

Pinckne

16

Mt.

Vernon St

Harvard Bridge

Charles River

Hatch Memo Shell

1

4

Lagoon

Storrow Drive

Gibson House Museum

PUBLIC GARDEN

Charles S

Storrow

Beacon St.

Clarendon St.

Berkeley St.

Arlington St.

Storrow Drive

Cushing Endicott House

BACK BAY

Dartmouth St.

Hunnewell Mansion

Emmanuel Church

St.

Boylston St

Church Court

Beacon St.

Ames-Webster Mansion

Commonwealth Av.

Newbury

ARLINGTON

Hereford St.

C.F. Adams House

Fairfield St.

Mass. Geneological Soc.

BAY VILLAGE

Ames Mansion

J.F. Andrew House

Fairfield St.

New Old South Church

Vendome

COPLEY

Copley Square

Trinity Church

James Av.

Columbu

Stuart St.

Beacon St.

Massachusetts Av.

Burrage Mansion

Newbury St.

Exeter St. Theatre

Boston Library

John Hancock Tower

Arlington St.

Commonwealth Av.

Institute of Contemporary Art

Boylston St.

Huntington Av.

Copley Place

Stuart St.

Plaza Castle Convention Center

Massachusetts TPK

Massachusetts TPK

AUDITORIUM

Dalton St.

Hynes Auditorium

Prudential Center

Buckingham St.

Columbus St.

Chandler

Berkeley St.

St.

Boylston St.

Hemenway St.

Massachusetts Av.

Belvidere St.

PRUDENTIAL

Carleton St.

Clarendon St.

Dartmouth St.

Bosten Center for the Arts

E. Berkele

BACK BAY FENS

Christian Science Center

Huntington Av.

Newton St.

SOUTH END

Harriet Tubman Park

Concord Baptist Church

Montgomery St.

to Museum of Fine Arts

to Holy Cross Cath.

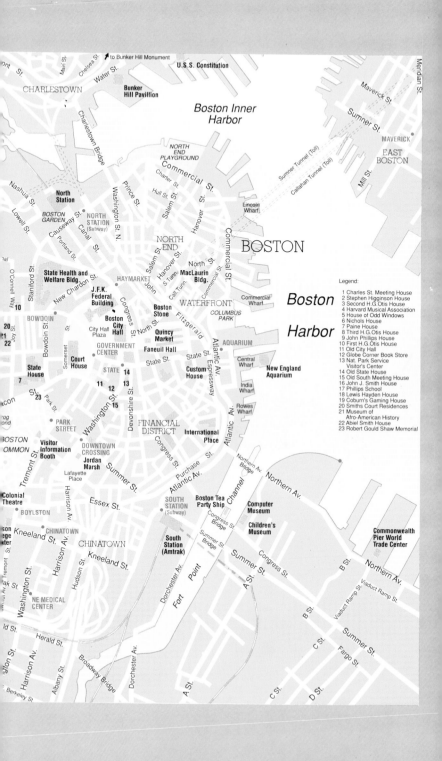

to Bunker Hill Monument

U.S.S. Constitution

CHARLESTOWN

Bunker
Hill Pavillion

*Boston Inner
Harbor*

Main St.
Chelsea St.
Water St.
Charlestown Bridge

NORTH
END
PLAYGROUND

Commercial St.

Charter St.
Hull St.
Salem St.

North St.

Nashua St.

North
Station

BOSTON
GARDEN

Lowell St.

Causeway St.

Portland St.

Canal St.

NORTH
STATION
(Subway)

Washington St. N.

Prince St.

Salem St.

Hanover St.

NORTH
END

Commercial St.

Lincoln
Wharf

BOSTON

Boston

Harbor

Commercial
Wharf

Sumner St.

Maverick St.

Meridian St.

Sumner St.

MAVERICK

EAST
BOSTON

Mill St.

Sumner Tunnel (Toll)

Callahan Tunnel (Toll)

O'Connell Way

Staniford St.

State Health and
Welfare Bldg.

New Chardon St.

J.F.K.
Federal
Building

HAYMARKET

Salem St.
Hanover St.
S.Turn.

North St.
MacLaurin
Bldg.

John St.

Call.Turn.

Congress St.

BOWDOIN

10

Bowdoin St.

Somerset St.

Boston
City Hall

City Hall Plaza

GOVERNMENT
CENTER

Boston
Stone

Quincy
Market

Faneuil Hall

WATERFRONT

COLUMBUS
PARK

Fitzgerald

Atlantic Av.

AQUARIUM

Central
Wharf

New England
Aquarium

India
Wharf

Rowes
Wharf

Legend:

1 Charles St. Meeting House
2 Stephen Higginson House
3 Second H.G.Otis House
4 Harvard Musical Association
5 House of Odd Windows
6 Nichols House
7 Paine House
8 Third H.G.Otis House
9 John Phillips House
10 First H.G.Otis House
11 Old City Hall
12 Globe Corner Book Store
13 Nat. Park Service
   Visitor's Center
14 Old State House
15 Old South Meeting House
16 John J. Smith House
17 Phillips School
18 Lewis Hayden House
19 Coburn's Gaming House
20 Smiths Court Residences
21 Museum of
   Afro-American History
22 Abiel Smith House
23 Robert Gould Shaw Memorial

20
21
22

State
House

7

23

Court
House

STATE

State St.

Custom
House

Atlantic Av. Espressway

Commercial St.

State St.

14
11 12
15
13

acon
rog
ond

Beacon St.
Park St.

PARK
STREET

BOSTON
COMMON

Tremont St.

Visitor
Information
Booth

Washington St.

Devonshire St.

FINANCIAL
DISTRICT

Congress St.

International
Place

DOWNTOWN
CROSSING

Jordan
Marsh

Lafayette
Place

Colonial
Theatre

BOYLSTON

Harrison Av.

Essex St.

Summer St.

Purchase St.

Atlantic Av.

Northern Av.
Bridge

Northern Av.

Computer
Museum

Children's
Museum

Commonwealth
Pier World
Trade Center

son
ege
ater

Kneeland St.

CHINATOWN

Harrison Av.

Hudson St.

CHINATOWN

Kneeland St.

SOUTH
STATION
(Subway)

South Station
Bridge

Congress St.
Bridge

Summer St.
Bridge

Boston Tea
Party Ship

Channel

Summer St.

Congress St.

Northern Av.

B St.

Tremont St.

ak St.

Washington St.

NE MEDICAL
CENTER

ld St.

Herald St.

Harrison Av.

Albany St.

Broadway Bridge

Dorchester Av.

Fort Point

South Station
(Amtrak)

A St.

Dorchester Av.

A St.

B St.

C St.

D St.

Viaduct Ramp St.

Viaduct Ramp St.

Summer St.

Fargo St.

Northern Av.

Berkeley St.

Day Itin

Boston, cradle of American independence, is small (population 580,000) and compact (40 square miles). It's a walker's city, with nearly all the attractions that visitors will want to enjoy contained within an area of about one square mile. Spreading out from this central neighborhood is Greater Boston,

Boston's finest

which consists of nearly 100 towns with a population of about 3 million. Cambridge, although separated from Boston by the Charles River, is inexorably linked with Boston and is a mere 10 minutes from downtown on the subway (MTBA or 'T').

Because of the convoluted roads and the Bostonians' blithe disregard for the law, driving is nerve-racking, and parking can be a problem. The subway is clean, safe and efficient. Worth getting is a 3- or 7-day MBTA Passport, which permits unlimited travel on the 'T', MBTA buses and on some rail zones, and which offers discounts at some attractions and restaurants.

The full-day and morning itineraries in the following pages are based on your being at the starting point at 9am, while afternoon itineraries 'start' at 2pm. Out-of-town itineraries are based on leaving the hotel at about 8.30am. All can be negotiated by public transportation and with some walking.

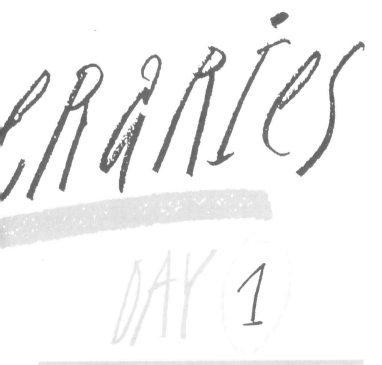

DAY 1

Freedom Trail, North End and Downtown

A 90-minute 'trolley' tour followed by a visit to the John Hancock Observatory provides an excellent introduction to the city. Follow this by a stroll through downtown.

– To the start: Inquire if the trolley bus stops at your hotel. If not, take the MBTA Green or Red Line to Park Street, or Blue Line to Aquarium or Green Line (B,C,D,E) to Copley Square, at each of which the trolley can be boarded –

The Freedom Trail is historic Boston's main tourist attraction, and for your first overview I will leave you in the hands and the commentary of the professionals. Three companies – **Beantown Trolley** (tel: 236-2148), **Brush Hill Tours** (tel: 720-6342) and **Old Town Trolley** (tel: 269-7010) – run identical, moderately priced, 6-mile trolley tours through Beacon Hill, the Back Bay, downtown, the waterfront

Copley Square

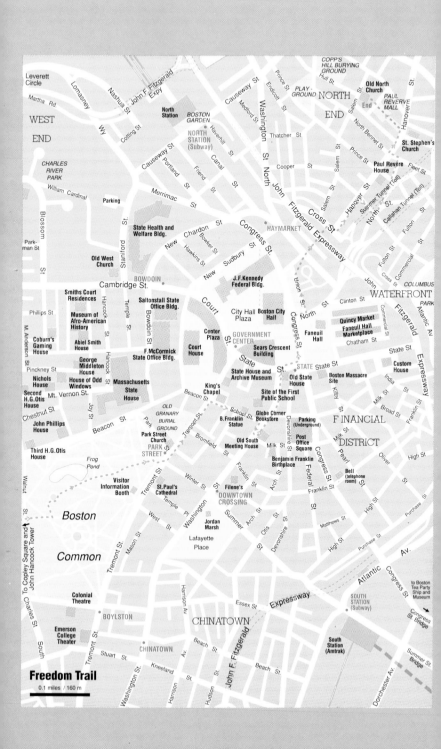

Leverett
Circle

Martha Rd.

Lomasney Wy

Nashua St

John F. Fitzgerald Expy

WEST
END

North
Station

BOSTON
GARDEN

Causeway St

Medford St

Prince St

Endicott St

Washington St

PLAY-GROUND

COPP'S
HILL BURYING
GROUND

Hull St

Old North
Church

Salem End

NORTH
END

PAUL
REVERVE
MALL

North St

Hanover St

CHARLES
RIVER
PARK

William Cardinal

Causeway St

Portland

Friend St

Canal St

Havenhill St

NORTH
STATION
(Subway)

Thatcher St

North St

Cooper St

Salem St

Prince St

North Bennet St

St. Stephen's
Church

Paul Revere
House

Fleet St

Merrimac St

Parking

Stanford St

State Health and
Welfare Bldg.

New

Chardon St

Bowker St

Sudbury St

Congress St

HAYMARKET

Union St

Cross St

John F. Fitzgerald Expressway

Summer Tunnel (Toll)

Callahan Tunnel (Toll)

North St

Fulton St

Commercial St

Cross St

Fulton St

Blossom St

Park-man St

Parkman St

Old West
Church

Stanford St

Hawkins St

New

BOWDOIN

Cambridge St.

J.F. Kennedy
Federal Bldg.

COLUMBUS

WATERFRONT
PARK

John F. Fitzgerald Expressway

Atlantic Av.

Phillips St

M. Anderson St

Smiths Court
Residences

Museum of
Afro-American
History

Hancock St

Temple St

Saltonstall State
Office Bldg.

Bowdoin St

Court St

City Hall
Plaza

Boston City
Hall

GOVERNMENT
CENTER

Clinton St

North St

Quincy Market
Faneuil Hall
Marketplace

Commercial St

Coburn's
Gaming
House

Abiel Smith
House

Center
Plaza

Sears Crescent
Building

Faneuil
Hall

Chatham St

State St

Custom
House

Pinckney St

George
Middleton
House

Hancock St

F.McCormick
State Office Bldg.

Court
House

State St

State St

State St

India St

Milk St

Broad St

Nichols
House

Second
H.G.Otis
House

Mt. Vernon St

Joy St

Massachusetts
State
House

King's
Chapel

Beacon St

State House and
Archive Museum

Old State
House

Site of the First
Public School

Boston Massacre
Site

Kilby St

FINANCIAL

Franklin St

Chestnut St

John Phillips
House

Beacon St

Park St

OLD
GRANARY
BURIAL
GROUND

Tremont St

School St

B.Franklin
Statue

Globe Corner
Bookstore

Devonshire St

Parking
(Underground)

Post
Office
Square

DISTRICT

Milk St

Pearl St

Oliver St

High St

Third H.G.Otis
House

Frog
Pond

Park Street
Church

PARK
STREET

Bromfield St

Old South
Meeting House

Milk St

Benjamin Franklin
Birthplace

Federal St

Congress St

Bell
(telephone
room)

High St

Walnut St

Visitor
Information
Booth

Tremont St

Winter St

St.Paul's
Cathedral

Temple Pl

Filene's

Franklin St

Arch St

Franklin St

High St

Purchase St

Boston
Common

Mason St

West St

Washington St

DOWNTOWN
CROSSING

Jordan
Marsh

Summer St

Arch St

Otis St

Devonshire St

Matthews St

High St

Purchase St

Atlantic Av.

Congress St

To Copley Square and
John Hancock Tower

To Charles St

Tremont St

Lafayette
Place

Harrison Av

SOUTH
STATION
(Subway)

Congress
St. Bridge

to Boston
Tea Party
Ship and
Museum

Colonial
Theatre

BOYLSTON

Tremont St

Essex St

Expressway

CHINATOWN

John F. Fitzgerald Expressway

Dorchester Av.

Summer St
Bridge

Emerson
College Theater

Stuart St

CHINATOWN

Kneeland St

Beach St

Beach St

Hudson St

South
Station
(Amtrak)

Washington St

Harrison

South St

Freedom Trail

0.1 miles / 160 m

and Charlestown, all passing close to many Freedom Trail sites. Uninterrupted tours last 90 minutes. However, passengers may get off as often as they wish and reboard a later trolley of the same company. The **Boston Tea Party Ship and Museum** (tel: 338-1773; daily 9am–5pm spring/6pm summer/5pm fall) is the only site not covered in other itineraries at which you might wish to stop.

Pick up this book again when you conclude your trolley ride at **Copley Square** near the blue, shimmering John Hancock Tower. However, before ascending, cross the road to the Skipjack restaurant. Adjacent to this is a pedestrian passage which hides the excellent **Caffe Gianni**. After ordering refreshments, find a seat in an impressive Parisian-style courtyard, where Gianni's has tables around two fountains.

After a snack, it's time to visit New England's tallest building, the **John Hancock Tower**. (From November to April the tower does not open until noon but a second opportunity to visit is offered in *Pick & Mix Option 2*). This glorious, rhomboidal structure from the drawing board of I M Pei had a somewhat inglorious birth in 1976. During its early years a wind torque caused more than one-third of the 10,000 glass panels which sheath the skyscraper to loosen and fall out. The John Hancock Mutual Life Insurance Company, not unnaturally, sued the contractors who sued the sub-contractors who sued the… However, all were insured with John Hancock.

Elevators whisk you to the 60th floor of this 740-ft building, where the sight

John Hancock Tower

of city landmarks and fantastic vistas stretching as far as New Hampshire are accompanied by the sonorous voice of the late Walter Muir Whitehill narrating a historical commentary. An added attraction is a mini sound-and-light show which features the defeat of the British in 1776. On descending from the skyscraper your next goal is Park Street Church at the intersection of Tremont and Park streets. If you're feeling tired, make for the in-bound entrance of the Copley Square MBTA station and get off after two stops at Park Street. A National Historic plaque at that station announces that this was where, in 1897, the country's first subway opened.

If you're feeling energetic, a 10-minute walk that will get you to the same destination and offer plenty of optional time for window-shopping follows: turn right, beyond Trinity Church, onto **Boylston Street** and, within three short blocks you will pass on the left Louis, Boston, *clothier par excellence*, in its own free-stand-

The view from John Hancock Tower

ing stately palace, and, on the right, FAO Schwartz, Shreve, Crump and Low (*the* Boston jewelers) and Hermès. At this point, cross Boylston Street and, on entering the **Public Garden**, swing right and walk along the pond, enjoying tantalizing glimpses of the famous Swan boats.

You'll arrive, after a furlong, at the Charles Street exit. Cross Charles Street and enter the **Common**, the oldest public park in the nation. Continue straight, ignoring the paths to the left, and pass the **Soldiers and Sailors Monument** honoring those who died in the Civil War. Beckoning is the **Park Street Church** (July and August from 10am–4pm) with its majestic Georgian steeple. William Lloyd Garrison made his first anti-slavery speech here in 1829, and in 1831 'America' was sung publicly for the first time. Immediately beyond this and hemmed in by buildings is the **Granary Burying Ground** (daily 8am–4pm), which contains the grave of patriot Paul Revere.

Paul Revere's tomb

Cross Tremont Street to reach, at the corner of School Street, the **Omni Parker House**, in which Charles Dickens participated in literary salons and Ho Chi Minh and Malcolm X reportedly waited on tables. This is also the birthplace of the Parker House roll and Boston cream pie. On the other side of School Street, in **Old City Hall**, an 1865 edifice in the French Second Empire style, is **Maison Robert** (tel: 227-3370), within which a modestly priced bistro lunch – salivate over the *tarte tatin* – can be enjoyed in **Ben's Café**. Here, patio dining is of-

24

fered alongside a bronze statue of Benjamin Franklin. Observe the *City Carpet* mosaic on the sidewalk outside the café. It commemorates the Boston Public Latin School, the first public school in the nation, founded on this site in 1635.

Continue down short School Street to the corner of Washington Street and the **Globe Corner Bookstore**, which was built in 1711. In the middle of the 19th century the building was a gathering place for Boston literati – 'the Exchange of Wit, the Rialto of current good things, the hub of the Hub' – including Longfellow, Holmes, Emerson and Hawthorne.

Immediately to the right on Washington Street, a nexus for downtown shops, is the spire of **Old South Meeting House** where, on December 16, 1773, more than 5,000 Boston citizens met to decide what to do with the three tea ships at Griffin's Wharf. They were determined that the heavily-taxed cargo of tea should not be unloaded. After a day-long meeting Samuel Adams proclaimed: 'This meeting can do nothing more to save the country!' Soon after, patriots disguised as Indians appeared at the door and, after a few whoops, ran down Milk Street to Griffin's Wharf. The crowd followed, and with cries of 'Boston harbor a teapot tonight!' 340 crates of tea were dumped into the water. Sitting in the pews of Old South, now an intriguing museum, and donning headphones, visitors are able to eavesdrop on this and other historical events which took place in the building.

The Old State House

On leaving Old South, turn right and, after a further 200 yards, turn right again on to **State Street**. Here is the **National Park Service Visitors' Center**, a valuable source of information and literature. Facing this is the **Old State House**, Boston's oldest public building, built in 1713. This was the seat of Colonial government until the Revolution; in 1787 John Hancock was inaugurated here as the first governor of the state under its new constitution. The building is readily recognizable by the brightly colored lion and unicorn, symbols of British imperial power. These symbols are replicas, however; the originals were tossed into the street when the Declaration of Independence was read from the balcony on July 18, 1776. The interior (9.30am–5pm, daily; tel: 720-3292) houses a museum.

From here, cross the road to **Congress Street,** stopping to observe the patterned cobblestones on the island with traffic lights. This marks the site of the **Boston Massacre**, which occurred on March 5, 1770, when five colonists, including one former slave, Crispus Attucks, were killed in a fracas involving British soldiers. A short distance north

Faneuil Hall

on Congress Street is the well-known **Faneuil Hall** (10am–9pm; tel: 248 0399). In the years that led to the Revolution this 'Cradle of Liberty' echoed to the patriotic rhetoric of James Otis, Samuel Adams and others. Liberty was also the keyword in 1837 when the mayor refused permission for an abolitionist meeting. Then Wendell Phillips thundered: 'When Liberty is in danger, Faneuil Hall has the right, it is her duty, to strike the key-note for the United States.' Competing with all this history is **Quincy Market**, adjacent to Faneuil Hall, but try to resist temptation; you'll be visiting here in *Pick & Mix Option 4*. (For anyone who cannot wait until lunchtime, the central building houses some 40 different eateries).

On leaving Faneuil Hall, enter short **Union Street**, which parallels and is separated by a small park from Congress Street. Here are two bronze statues, one seated and one standing, of James Curley, the quintessential Irish politician who dominated Boston politics from 1920 to 1950 and was even re-elected while in jail. To the right is the **Union Oyster House** (tel: 227-2750) where, in 1776, the exiled Louis Philippe, a future king of France, eked out a living teaching French and where Daniel Webster threw back raw oysters and drank brandy. You might wish to have lunch at the excellent raw bar.

Turning right at the Oyster House, follow tiny Marshall Street across Blackstone Street and through an underpass below the freeway. Once you exit, you're in the **North End**, or **Little Italy**, near **Hanover Street**, the district's main artery. A couple of hundred yards along Hanover Street, on the right, is Richmond Street, which leads to Garden Court and the **Paul Revere House** (summer 9.30am– 5.15pm; winter 11am–4.15pm, closed Monday in January, February and March; tel: 523-1676). The oldest house in the city, it was built in 1676 and by the time it was purchased by Paul Revere in 1770 had been considerably altered. The building is furnished much as it was when it was home to Paul and the first Mrs Revere, who bore him no less than eight children. When she died, the sec-

Beaver II, the Tea Party ship

Paul Revere's House

ond Mrs Revere bore him a similar brood.

Continuing past the Revere House, turn left onto Fleet Street, which will return you to Hanover Street. A right turn here and, on the right, is **St Stephen's Church**, the only church by architect Charles Bulfinch still standing in Boston. To the left is the wide **Prado**, or **Paul Revere Mall**. Here stands an equestrian statue of the great man.

A stroll along the mall leads to the rear of **Christ Church**, also known as **Old North Church** (9am–5pm; tel: 523 6676). It was on the night of April 18, 1775, that the sexton, on instructions from Paul Revere, hung two lanterns from the 197-ft high steeple to alert patriots in Charlestown that the British were advancing to Concord by boat from Boston Common – 'one, if by land, and two, if by sea.' In 1860, Henry Wadsworth Longfellow, on climbing the steeple, was inspired to write the poem *Paul Revere's Ride*. Today's steeple is a 1955 reproduction. The original was knocked down in an 1806 hurricane and the replacement by another in 1954.

Cambridge and Harvard

Exploring old Cambridge and Harvard University, mostly the college and its museums. The art museums are closed on Monday.

– To the start: MBTA *Red Line to Harvard Square or bus route 1 along Massachusetts Avenue to Harvard Square –*

First, orient yourself in **Harvard Square**, which is an amorphous area rather than a true square. This is most easily done by identifying **The Coop**, or Harvard Cooperative Society, a department store founded in 1882. The Coop lies to the west. To the East is **Harvard Yard**, containing the university's most historic buildings, bordered on the south and the west by Massachusetts Avenue.

Enter Harvard Yard by the Johnston

27

Harvard Square

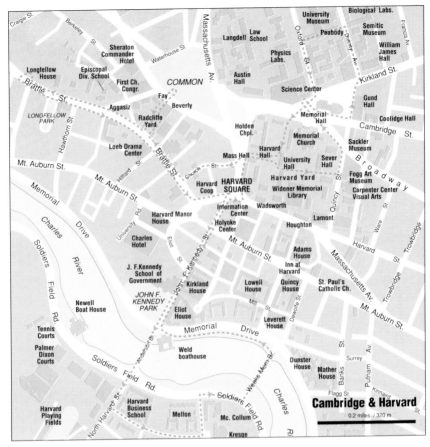

Gate, which is on the west arm of Massachusetts Avenue. Immediately to the right after you pass through the gate is ivy-covered **Massachusetts Hall** (1720); on the left is Harvard Hall (1766). Observe on the western gable of the former – the oldest Harvard building still standing today – the **College Clock**, part of the original structure. It is painted to resemble its 18th-century appearance. During the Revolutionary War Continental Army soldiers were billeted here. **Harvard Hall** is the third college building to stand on this site. The original was razed by a fire in 1764 which was called 'the greatest disaster in the history of the College,' destroying as it did the largest library in the colonies, including John Harvard's own collection of books.

Facing you across the grass is **University Hall**, an 1816 granite building designed by Bulfinch. It now houses university offices but origi-

The Statue of Three Lies

Widener Library and Memorial Church

nally contained dining rooms, classrooms, a chapel and the president's office. The bronze statue of John Harvard in front of University Hall is often nicknamed *The Statue of Three Lies*, because the statue is not of John Harvard but of an undergraduate in 1884, the year the figure was sculpted by Daniel French Chester; the inscription refers to John Harvard as founder of Harvard College, when he was in fact only the first major benefactor; it also mistakenly notes that the College was founded in 1638, the year of the John Harvard bequest. It was actually founded in 1636.

Walk past University Hall into the **Tercentenary Quadrangle** or **New Yard** which, on the first Monday of each June, is the scene of Commencement. This yard is dominated on the south by **Widener Memorial Library's** massive Corinthian colonnade atop a monumental flight of stairs and, on the north, by the soaring, delicate, white spire of **Memorial Church**, which honors the Harvard dead in both world wars. The rear (east) of University Hall, almost as handsome as the front, faces Richardson's Romanesque **Sever Hall**, which has been called 'a turning point in the course of American architecture.' Its entrance is flanked by turreted towers and the entire building is rich in decorative brickwork.

Enter the Widener which, with 56 miles of shelves, is the third largest library in the whole of the nation but still only part of the largest university library in the world which runs to 13 million volumes. The **Memorial Room**, a handsome affair of wood paneling and stained-glass windows, contains the private library of Harry Widener, a young Harvard bibliophile who drowned in the sinking of the *Titanic*, and includes a Gutenberg Bible and a first folio of Shakespeare. Bibliophiles should also pay a visit to the adjacent **Houghton Library** (Monday to Friday 9am–5pm), to admire a brilliant collection of early books, including the only surviving volume from the Harvard Hall fire.

Exhibit in Fogg Museum

Leaving the New Yard by the gate across from Sever Hall, emerge on **Quincy Street** where you will find yourself facing the **Fogg Museum**, the most famous of Harvard's nine museums. Although these superbly stocked museums are all open to

Fall in the Harvard Yard

the public, their primary purpose is not to entertain the casual visitor but to educate Harvard students. It is impossible to do justice to them all in one day. You must therefore decide if you prefer a 'once-over' of all or to concentrate on the three art museums or the four natural history museums. (The Semitic Museum and the Scientific Instruments Collection are of specialist appeal.) Whatever your decision, the time allocated for museum visits on today's excursion is about 2 hours.

The Fogg, Werner Otto Hall (a 1991 extension behind the Fogg), and the Sackler, immediately north of the Fogg, are the three art museums. Before entering the museums, turn right for a few paces to admire the striking modern **Carpenter Center for the Visual Arts**, the only Le Corbusier building in North America.

Highlights in the Fogg (Monday to Saturday 10am–5pm, Sunday 1–5pm; tel: 495-9400) include the Ingres paintings, and a splendid assembly of French Impressionist and Pre-Raphaelite works. In addition, there are dozens of Blake watercolors and a print room with hundreds of Dürers and Rembrandts. Lovers of German art will delight in the Busch-Reisinger collection, in the **Werner Otto Hall**. Outstanding are the 20th-century Expressionist canvases by Klee and Kandinsky. Ecclesiastical sculpture, 18th-century rococo porcelain, jewelry, textiles, furniture and metal crafts are also on display. Here, too, are the archives of Gropius and Feininger in the largest Bauhaus collection outside Germany.

Now is the time to address the question of coffee. At this hour

The Science Center, Harvard's largest building

Harvard Science Center

the choice is limited, so become a Harvard student by turning left onto Broadway, just outside the Fogg, and walking for about 150 yards to arrive at a plaza where the Tanner Fountain plays in front of the large, white, glass-and-concrete **Science Center**, the largest of all Harvard buildings. Inside is an attractive courtyard where you can take a coffee break.

Refreshed, backtrack to Quincy Street where, across the road from the Fogg, is the **Sackler**, a wonderful museum of modest size containing what many claim is the world's most outstanding collection of Chinese jades. Its Ancient and Islamic collections are also noteworthy. Continuing north on Quincy Street, cross Cambridge Street and observe on the left **Memorial Hall**, a huge, reddish, Gothic-Ruskinian pile with polychromatic roofs, which contains the largest auditorium in the university, **Sanders Theater**. Its somewhat truncated appearance is the result of a fire in which the tall pinnacled roof over the central tower was destroyed. If the building is open, go in to admire the windows, which are a veritable museum of American stained glass. On the right of Memorial Hall is slender-pillared **Gund Hall**, home of the Graduate School of Design.

A Redcoat on parade

Cross Kirkland Street and enter Divinity Avenue, which is guarded on one side by the handsome medieval **Adolph Busch Hall**, which owes its name to the beer baron, and on the other by the **William James Hall** skyscraper, home to the Behavioral Science Department. At the end of this short street are the **Museums of Natural History** (Monday to Saturday 9am–4.30pm, Sunday 1pm–4.30pm; tel: 495-1910), of which the best known is the **Peabody** (which, incidentally, has an excellent gift shop). The most famous exhibits are the **Glass Flowers**, handmade glass plants copied from nature with an extraordinary attention to detail. They are not, however, to everyone's taste: the Glass Flowers top *Boston Globe* travel writer William Davis's list of the 'Five Worst Travel Attractions in the Western Hemisphere.'

Exit the natural history museums on Oxford Street and, turning left, return to the Science Center. At the far side of the plaza, reenter Harvard Yard. After passing Holworthy, Hollis, Stoughton and Thayer, all of which are freshman dormitories, you'll find your-

The Longfellow House

self in familiar territory. Exit by the Johnston Gate. Facing the gate, on the other side of Massachusetts Avenue, is 200-yard-long Church Street, which debouches into Brattle Street, where lunch awaits at number 44, **The Harvest**. Here, at moderate prices, contemporary New England cuisine is served in a variety of rooms and on the patio. Next door is the **Harvest Express**, where you can pick up the makings of a picnic to enjoy in Radcliffe Yard, which is about 100 yards farther along on the opposite side of Brattle.

Less expensive eateries with a Cambridge tradition are found on either side of The Harvest. **Casablanca**, at No 40, serves Mediterranean cuisine in two rooms covered with murals from the movie.

Au Bon Pain

At No 56 is the **Blacksmith House Bakery Café** where, if not 'Under a Spreading Chestnut Tree' but at least on a leafy patio, light lunches including superb Viennese pastries can be savored. Dexter Pratt, the smithy in Longfellow's poem, *The Village Blacksmith*, lived in this yellow, hip-roofed house, which dates from 1811.

After lunch, spare a glance for the handsome, modern **Loeb Drama Center**, at 66 Brattle Street, which is home to the American Repertory Theater. Then, cross the road and stroll through **Radcliffe Yard**, which is surrounded by a number of delightful late 19th- and early 20th-century buildings. This is where the renowned ladies' college of that name, now fully integrated with Harvard, began life in 1879. Exit from the far side of the yard onto Garden Street which borders **Cambridge Common**, a treasure trove of markers, memorials and monuments. Slightly to the right, surrounded by a semi-circle of cannon, stands a bronze relief marking the spot where, on July 4, 1775, George Washington assumed command of the Continental Army.

Back on Brattle and proceeding out of town, you will soon see why this is the most prestigious street in Cambridge. All the hubbub is gone and the leafy, tranquil street is lined by splendid clapboard houses fronted by elegant porticoes, most from the 19th century but some from the 18th. Many bear plaques commemorating the greats who have lived in them.

The most famous, the **Henry Wadsworth Longfellow House** (daily 10am–4.30pm, but call in advance as in recent years the museum has been closed between November and the end of April; tel: 876-4491), is the yellow clapboard building at No 105. Longfellow arrived here as a lodger in 1837, received the house as a wedding gift from his father-in-law and remained in the building until 1882. The gardens, old carriage house and the house – virtually as it was in Longfellow's time, with memorabilia including a chair made from the 'spreading chestnut tree' – can be visited.

Harvard Square

From here, stroll back along Brattle Street toward Harvard Square for coffee under shady trees at **Au Bon Pain**, a busy self-service café. This is the place to watch the Harvard Square world go by. Alternatively, walk south from the square on John F Kennedy (JFK) Street and enter **The Garage** shopping complex at the corner of Mount Auburn Street. Here is the **Coffee Connection**, which has the largest selection of coffees in Greater Boston.

Continuing on JFK Street you will pass **Kirkland** and then **Eliot House**, neo-Georgian Harvard College residential houses. Each co-educational house, of which there are now 13, is a small college in its own right with about 400 students; herein lies much of the strength of Harvard College. Each house has its own administration and a phalanx of tutors; its own library and dining hall; its own societies and clubs. The concept of the houses came from Edward Harkness, a Yale alumnus who, spurned by his *alma mater,* donated $13.8 million to Harvard in 1929 for the original seven houses.

On the other side of JFK Street, facing Kirkland and Eliot Houses, are the buildings of Harvard's **J F Kennedy School of Government**, where the world's great statespeople appear to lecture, to debate, to pontificate at 'The Forum,' a program of panel discussions on public affairs and problems hosted by the school's Institute of Politics. A mere 500 yards from the square is the Charles River. Cross

The Weld Boathouse

the **Larz Anderson Bridge**, pausing to admire the superb views of the college and, in the foreground, the **Weld Boathouse**, home of Harvard's women's crew. The boathouse to the right is home to the men's crew.

Having crossed the river, continue straight on what is now Boylston Street, for 150 yards, passing on the right the playing fields of Harvard and, on the left, **Harvard Business School**, the most prestigious business school in the world. Turn left and stroll through the campus with its neo-Georgian buildings which display a consistent rhythm of green doors, white window-frames and red-brick walls. Soon, you'll be back at the river. A right turn leads, after 200 yards, to the **John W Weeks Footbridge**, which offers an excellent view of some of Harvard's residential buildings.

DAY 3

The Public Garden and Beacon Hill

Beacon Hill is a National Historic Landmark. The hill is also the location of many of the sights on Boston's Black Heritage Trail. The day also includes a swan boat ride and a visit to the State House.

– To the start: MBTA Green Line (B,C,D,E) to Arlington Street –

Of all the neighborhoods in traditional Boston, Beacon Hill is the most unswervingly traditional. Although Beacon Hill is invariably associated with wealthy 'Boston Brahmins,' it has always attracted a diverse population whose Bohemian members resided on the north or 'bad' side – the derogatory term refers to the social standing of the residents – rather than on the sunny south side. Beacon Hill is also the only downtown area of any large American city that has been residential since its founding.

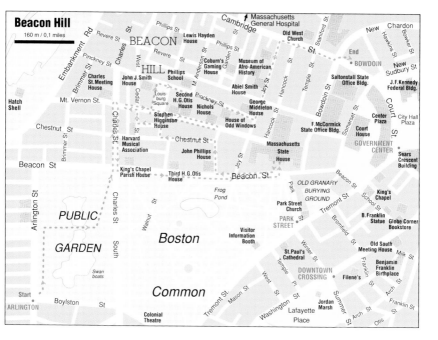

Beacon Hill

160 m / 0,1 miles

On emerging from the subway onto Arlington Street, cross the road and enter the glorious **Public Garden**, the oldest botanical garden in the country. Although it is not large, you cannot help but delight in its magnificently maintained formal flower beds and its lovely pond bordered by weeping willows. Walk along the path which parallels Arlington Street to arrive at a splendid equestrian statue of George Washington who, according to Thomas Jefferson, was the best horseman of his age.

Now turn right and arrive at the mock suspension bridge over the pond. Here is the dock for the **swan boats**, which have been a constant spring-to-fall feature of the Boston scene since the Paget family (who still run them) introduced the boats in 1877. Unfortunately, the first boat does not leave until 10am and so you will have to postpone the joys of a leisurely, inexpensive 15-minute voyage until after lunch. Having crossed the bridge, turn left and make your way to the gate, diagonally opposite the one previously entered, at the corner of Charles and Beacon streets. You are now at the southwest corner of Beacon Hill.

Charles Street, the commercial hub of the hill, is lined with antique shops and art galleries, bakeries and bookstores, boutiques and eateries. A couple of hundred yards along on the left is the former **Charles Street Meeting House**, now a complex of offices and stores. Readily recognizable by its lantern tower and clock, it was purchased by the African Methodist Episcopalian Church and, in 1939, was

Swan boat in the Public Garden

35

A snack in the park

the last black institution to leave Beacon Hill.

Before continuing, pause for a light brunch at **Il Dolce Momento**, at the corner of Charles and Chestnut streets, or across the road at **Romano's Bakery**, 89 Charles Street, a downstairs eatery which tends to be less crowded and more reasonably priced. Romano's is especially enjoyable during winter, when they stoke up the fire.

Backtrack on Charles, turn left and ascend **Beacon**, which was described by Oliver Wendell Holmes as 'the sunny street that holds the sifted few.' The **Common** is to the right and some of the grandest Beacon Hill buildings, many now clubs, are to the left. A plaque at No 50, at the corner of **Spruce Street**, remembers the Reverend Blackstone who was the original Bostonian, having come to live at this spot in about 1625. Several years later Blackstone invited the Puritans to leave disease-ridden Charlestown, where they had settled, and to come to where the water was purer. The invitation was accepted and he sold them all but 6 acres of the peninsula that he had purchased from the Indians.

The Federal-style building at No **45**, solid and square, and topped by a balustrade, was built in 1806 by Charles Bulfinch for Harrison Gray Otis. Bulfinch, a Bostonian, was the foremost architect in America in the first decades after the Revolution; Otis was Boston's third mayor, and this was his third Bulfinch house in 9 years. The house is now occupied by the **American Meteorological Society**, and the terms of their lease require them to show the splendid interior to anyone who rings the bell. I recommend that you do just that.

Next door, at **No 42**, the glistening-white granite building with two large bow windows belongs to the exclusive **Somerset Club**, which, when it suffered a fire, demanded that firemen use the tradesmen's entrance. At Nos 40 and 39, observe the purple windows, a badge of age cherished beyond belief. The color appeared because an 1818 shipment of glass from Hamburg contained traces of manganese oxide which, after years of exposure to sunlight, darkened to a deep purple hue.

At the crest of the hill, cross the road to

admire the **Robert Gould Shaw Memorial**, which honors the very first regiment of freed blacks in the Civil War. The regiment, which was raised in Boston, was led by white officers under 26-year-old Robert Gould Shaw. A member of this unit, Sergeant William Carney, was the first African American to win the Congressional Medal of Honor. The relief depicts the regiment's farewell march down Beacon Street past the residence of Shaw's family at No 44.

Across the road from the Shaw Memorial is the magnificent **State House** (tel: 727-3676; frequent 45-minute guided tours) which is open Monday to Friday 10am–4pm. This, the outstanding public building in the country for decades after its construction, is the most famous building designed by Bulfinch. Originally, the gilded dome was covered with shingles, but in 1802 Paul Revere sheathed it in copper. In 1861, it was crowned in its present glory, in gold leaf.

Inside, beneath the dome, are the Doric Hall, a vaulted columned marble hall with a statue of Washington, and the Hall of Flags, in which the colors of state military units are displayed. A double

The State House

JFK Memorial at the State House

stairway climbs to the chamber of the House of Representatives, an impressive, oval-shaped room in which hangs the *Sacred Cod*, a gilded, carved-wood representation of the staple diet of the first settlers and later a mainstay of both Boston's and Massachusetts' economy. On leaving the front of the State House, turn right to admire in the gardens a life-sized statue of John F Kennedy.

So far you've only explored the periphery of Beacon Hill, but if you walk back down Beacon for 100 yards and turn right onto Walnut Street, you will enter the heart of the hill. Here, streets are narrower and bordered by elegant blocks of red-brick townhouses that blend together harmoniously. These are enhanced by delightful minimal ornamentation in the form of wrought-iron railings, fences and boot-scrapers; slender columns flanking doorways; and delicate fanlights. More examples can be seen if you turn left onto and then descend **Chestnut Street**. Bulfinch enthusiasts will be especially impressed by Nos 13, 15, 17 and 29A; the latter is the oldest home on the South slope.

Near the bottom of Chestnut, turn right onto Willow Street and then immediately left onto cobbled, steep **Acorn Street**, one of the gems of the hill. Acorn ends in West Cedar Street, where, not that long ago, furious residents sat down on this walkway to save all the hill's brick sidewalks from being removed in the name of progress. A right turn here leads to **Mount Vernon Street** where, at No 119, is **Another Season** (tel: 367 0880), a delightful restaurant popular with local residents. Request a table in the front room and enjoy a slightly expensive, eclectic and constantly changing international menu. For a faster, less expensive meal, descend a few more yards onto Charles Street and return to Il Dolce Momento or Romano's Bakery. A middle course could be taken by lunching at **Rebecca's** at 21 Charles Street (tel: 742-9747), where you can enjoy a splendid view both of the kitchen and the passing energetic street scene.

Alternatively, if the weather cooperates, you could cross the road to **Rebecca's** café at the Charles Street Meeting House and, laden with delicious goodies, picnic at the nearby Public Garden, after which you can enjoy that voyage aboard the swan boats.

This could be a good time to visit the **Bull & Finch** pub, the model for the TV sitcom

Chestnut Street

38

Acorn Street

Cheers, at 84 Beacon Street (tel: 227-9605), opposite the Public Garden, for a cold one and a hamburger. For reasons that are beyond me – and I enjoy the TV program – this is one of Boston's top three tourist attractions. Be prepared for long lines, and not that much to see once you are inside.

After lunch, begin the ascent up steep and leafy Mount Vernon Street. Ignore for the moment the magic of Louisburg Square and concentrate on Mount Vernon, which Henry James claimed was 'the only respectable street in America.' Especially interesting is No **85**, the **Second Harrison Gray Otis House** which, standing alone, is an exception to Beacon Hill's dense development. This Bulfinch building represents his vision of Mount Vernon Street which he had hoped would be lined by grand, free-standing mansions, each in its own spacious grounds. Daniel Webster lived for a time at No 57 and Henry Adams, who refused a job at Harvard because he knew 'nothing of history, less about teaching, and too much about Harvard,' spent his boyhood here.

Now you can make for **Louisburg Square** (the 'S' is pronounced). A small, iron-fenced park in the middle of the square, which is exclusively for the use of those who reside here, is surrounded by a cobblestone street that is flanked by facing rows of dignified, red-brick houses. An undistinguished statue of Columbus stands at the north end of the park, while the equally undistinguished figure at the south end is of Aristides the Just, a 5th-century Athenian statesman. The bowfronted houses on the left, from No 10 to the far (north) end, are the most handsome and have, in the past, been lauded as the most splendid row of houses in the United States.

When William Dean Howells was editor of the *Atlantic Monthly*, he lived at No 4. Louisa May Alcott's literary success enabled her to purchase No. 10 and move from the 'bad' side of the hill with her penniless parents and sisters. But

then Beacon Hill has always been home to Boston literati; others who have lived here include Nathaniel Hawthorne, John P. Marquand and Julia Ward Howe, author of the stirring *Battle Hymn of the Republic*.

Exiting from the north side of the square, you come to **Pinckney Street**, which, with **Myrtle Street**, the parallel street to the north, is the dividing line between the dignified south slope and the more Bohemian 'north' slope. This was the address of many literary figures and, in the 19th century, was home to a thriving African American community. The red-brick condominium building at the corner of Anderson Street was once the **Phillips School** which, when opened to African Americans in 1855, became the city's first interracial school. Across from the school, at No 62, is one of sev-

Cheers at the Bull & Finch

eral houses on Beacon Hill which were stopping points on the 'underground railway' which helped fugitive slaves on their way to freedom in Canada.

A handsome home which belonged to John J Smith, a distinguished African American statesman who migrated to Boston from Virginia in 1848, is at No 68 Pinckney. Stationed in Washington during the Civil War, John J Smith was a recruiting officer for the all-black Fifth Cavalry. Subsequently, he was thrice appointed to the Massachusetts House of Representatives, then later to the Boston Common Council.

Further along, at No 24, is the **House of Odd Windows**. It is exactly that. The Alcotts lived at No 20 Pinckney Street before striking it rich and moving to Louisburg Square. Across the road is the delightful No 9, which is an iron gate guarding a tunnel that passes through a house into a hidden courtyard surrounded by three houses. The hill abounds with such treasures.

Turn left onto Joy Street, one of the oldest streets in Boston; walk 150 yards past Myrtle Street and arrive at tiny **Smith Court**, at the corner of which stood the **Abiel Smith School**, dedicated in 1834 to the education of the city's African American children. At one time all the houses in Smith Court were occupied by African Americans. Facing these houses is the **African Meeting House**, the oldest African American church in the nation still standing. Dedicated in 1806, it was called 'the

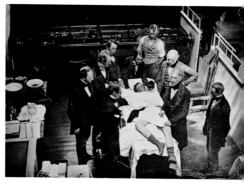

First use of ether at the General Hospital

haven from the loft' because of the practice in Old North Church of relegating African American worshippers to the loft. It was also called 'Black Faneuil Hall' because of fiery anti-slavery meetings held here. These culminated in 1832 when William Lloyd Garrison founded the New England Anti-Slavery Society. In his words: 'Faneuil Hall shall ere long echo with the principles we have set forth. We shall shake the nation by their mighty power.'

Continue down Joy Street, which soon merges into Cambridge Street. A short distance to the left is the **Massachusetts General Hospital**, where, in 1846, ether was used for the first time to anaesthetize a patient. Slightly to the right is the **First Harrison Gray Otis House**, now owned by the Society for the Preservation of New England Antiquities, and, alongside it, the **Old West Church**, whose predecessor was razed in the Revolutionary War by the British, who thought that the Americans were using it to signal to their compatriots in Cambridge.

A few yards farther on, just beyond New Chardon Street, is the MBTA Bowdoin station, which offers a speedy return route.

PICK &

Morning Itineraries

1. The Back Bay

Newbury Street

The Back Bay is a perfect grid and the streets running from north to south are named alphabetically. Newbury Street is *the* shopping street in Boston.

– To the start: MBTA Green Line (B,C,D,E) to Arlington Street –

The Back Bay, composed of landfill, is a living record of late 19th century architectural styles in America. This was *the* address in the city until the Depression. Then degentrification set in and grand aristocratic homes were converted into apartments and dormitories for the city's many colleges. However, with the condominium craze of the 1970s, parts of Back Bay regained their former glory and Beacon Street is again, as in bygone days, home to the rich, although generally the new rather than the old.

To begin a tour, walk north on Arlington Street, passing the brownstone church of that name, to arrive at Newbury Street. This is one of five streets (the others are Boylston, Commonwealth, Marlborough, Beacon), each with a somewhat different character, which run the length of the Back Bay. The **Ritz-Carlton Hotel**, a quintessential Boston institution, at the corner of Arlington and Newbury, is still Boston's finest. The romantic tradition

MIX

Newbury Street dining

of rooftop dining and dancing has recently been resumed here.

At the Arlington (Public Garden) end, Newbury Street is occupied by chic stores of a rather intimidating mien, with prices to match. The street is justly renowned for its dozens of galleries and antique stores, and scores of upscale clothing stores; interspersed among these are an array of inviting sidewalk cafés and restaurants. This being Boston, there are bookstores and ice-cream parlors galore. More ice-cream is consumed per capita in Boston than anywhere else in the nation.

Shopping begins with a bang with the Ritz-Carlton's neighbors on the first block. These include Burberry's, Brooks Brothers and Cartier. Then, at the corner of Berkeley Street comes **Louis, Boston** which occupies a free-standing 1863 French Academic Manse which was originally the New England Museum of Natural History. A

The Back Bay and Charles River

Time out for shopping

visit to this men's store, which also has a women's division, is a must: though the prices can be outrageous, the service is impeccable.

Continue on Newbury until the intersection with Clarendon and then turn right. The lovely tower that soars above Commonwealth Avenue, where we are headed, belongs to H H Richardson's **First Baptist Church**. The tower's frieze was modeled in Paris by Auguste Bartholdi, who sculpted the Statue of Liberty. The faces in it are said to be likenesses of noted Bostonians, including Longfellow, Emerson, and Hawthorne. The trumpeting angels on the corners have earned the building the sobriquet of the 'Church of the Holy Bean Blowers.'

For the moment, ignore Commonwealth Avenue and continue on Clarendon to Marlborough, a street whose architecture is somewhat more homogeneous than elsewhere in the Back Bay; mansard roofs and bow windows are common features and the gas lamps lend an old-fashioned air. The next street over is Beacon, where a right turn passes Nos 150 and 170, two splendid Italian Renaissance Revival buildings with rusticated first floors. The former is where the Gardners (of the Gardner Museum) resided: the latter is home to the Goethe Institute.

On reaching Arlington Street, turn right and then enter **Commonwealth Avenue**, which is the *pièce de résistance* of the Back Bay. A 100-ft-wide shady mall which shelters half a dozen interesting statues runs down the middle of this broad, French-inspired

Newbury Street gallery

boulevard. Many handsome buildings now owned by institutes, such as No 5 (the Boston Center for Adult Education) and No 21 (Emerson College) were once private homes. The interiors of these buildings give ample opportunity to 'ah' and to 'oh' at the grandeur of some of Boston's former residences. The grandest houses, such as the **Hooper Mansion** at No 25–7 (northwest corner of Berkeley) occur at the corners of blocks.

But shopping calls and so, on reaching Clarendon, turn left for a block and then right back onto Newbury, where grand stores are interspersed with long-established art galleries. Homage should now be paid to the sidewalk cafés. **Café Florian** (85 Newbury), Boston's oldest and most authentic coffee house, is one of my favorites. Then, there is the almost ubiquitous and always dependable **Coffee Connection** at No 165.

Spare a glance, at the corner of Exeter Street, for the **Ames-Webster** mansion (No 306), which generally receives the accolade of the most glorious building in the Back Bay. The imposing brownstone and granite mass is still, for many, the Exeter Street Theater. Built in 1884 as a temple for the Working Union of Progressive Spiritualists, it was converted into a movie house in 1914 and reigned as an art cinema for over 60 years. It is now occupied by Waterstone's, a British bookstore.

In the next block, on the left, the elegant Emporio Armani has taken up residence. As you head toward the far end of Newbury Street, beyond the intersection of Fairfield, the stores become progressively funkier and more youth-oriented: for cutting-edge clothes, check out Culture Shock at No 286. The buildings in the last block, between Hereford and Massachusetts Avenue, were once coach houses, yet the street ends with a flourish with a grand renovated building which is home to **Tower Records Video**, which claims to be one of the largest music stores in the world.

At this corner turn right and walk along an undistinguished part of busy Massachusetts Avenue to the far side of **Commonwealth Avenue**, where a large brownstone mansion, modeled after a 16th-century French château, stands. The **Oliver Ames** mansion, the largest in the Back Bay, is now part of Emerson College and if you enter you can again admire the stately interior of a grand Back Bay home.

*John Hancock Tower
and the First Baptist Church*

Prudential Center

Three outstanding buildings occupy corners at the intersection of Commonwealth and Hereford. The **Andrews Mansion** (32 Hereford), which was the first Italian Renaissance Revival-style building in the Back Bay, is now occupied and beautifully maintained by an MIT fraternity. Cross the avenue to 40 Hereford, where Georgian replaces Renaissance in the house where Fannie Merritt Farmer founded her well-known school of cookery. Across the road from this, at 314 Commonwealth, is the exuberant, flamboyant **Burrage Mansion**, where ornamentation runs wild. Boston, 'home of the bean and the cod,' is forgotten here.

Now turn right onto Gloucester. Beckoning from Boylston Street, a few giant steps away, is the soaring tower of the **Prudential Center**, known to all as 'The Pru.' When the center was being built in the early 1960s, it was hailed as the harbinger of the 'New Boston.' Elevators shoot the visitor in seconds to the **Skywalk** on the 50th floor, for a fantastic panorama of the city.

2. Around Copley Square

An architectural primer with shopping and a visit to the Christian Science Complex.

– To the start: MBTA Green Line (B,C,D,E) to Copley Square –

After an unsuccessful stab at modernization, **Copley Square**, a focal point of Boston, was restored in 1989 to a more low-key, traditional look – a more suitable backdrop for the masterworks of

Trinity Church reflected in John Hancock Tower

19th- and 20th-century American architecture that surround it.

The most renowned building in the square is **Trinity Church**, a seminal work in American architecture which initiated the Romanesque Revival. It occupies the east side of the square and is open daily from 8am–6pm. Enter through the west porch which leads into a bright, almost dazzling, richly decorated interior. The superb frescoes are the work of John La Farge who also supervised the stained-glass windows. Especially noteworthy are the three turquoise lancet windows above the porch.

Cross the square to the **Boston Public Library**, a massive Renaissance Revival pile designed by Charles Follen McKim. Although it is now generally acclaimed as a masterpiece, when finished in 1895 it was dismissed as a 'warehouse' and compared to the city morgue. Ascend the steps of the library (tel: 536-5400), which opens Monday to Saturday at 9am and on Sunday, except from June to September, at 2pm, and enter through three magnificent pairs of bronze doors with allegorical bas reliefs. Representing music and poetry, knowledge and wisdom, truth and romance, these are the work of Daniel

Flowers in Copley Square

Chester French, the sculptor of the Lincoln Memorial in Washington. Observe the words 'Free for All' inscribed above the entrance: founded in 1852, this is the oldest free municipal library in the world.

Inside, ascend the stairway which Henry James hailed for 'its splendid tawny marble' to the second floor to view one of the library's unequaled murals, a painting of the *Nine Muses* by Puvis de Chavannes. On the right is a reading room modeled after the library of the Doges' Palace in Venice. The New Wing exit leads through a central cloistered courtyard, which, with its shady trees and bubbling fountain, offers a tranquil haven far from the crowds. Art-lovers and bibliophiles might wish to linger by joining one of the 60-minute tours which depart from the main desk in the New Wing. (Monday 2.30pm, Tuesday and Wednesday 6.30pm, Thursday to Saturday 11am).

On leaving the library, cross Boylston Street for a refreshment at **Geoffrey's Cafe-Bar** (tel: 437-6400) recognizable in the summer from its cluster of umbrellas. A few steps beyond this, toward Copley Square, is the striking North Italian Gothic campanile of **New Old South Church**. Diagonally across Copley Square from the

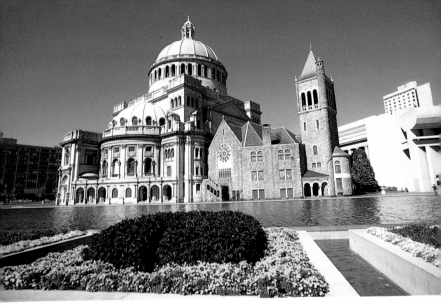

The Christian Science Complex

church is the gleaming glass **John Hancock Tower**. Now is the time to visit the latter if you omitted to do so on *Day 1*.

Descending from the Hancock Tower, turn left, pass the elegant bow-fronted, Renaissance-style **Copley Plaza Hotel**, cross Dartmouth Street and enter the modern **Westin Hotel**, which is part of **Copley Place**, Boston's largest and most expensive private development. Ascend the escalator, past a waterfall, to the hotel lobby. Continue straight through and arrive at two floors of stores surrounding a nine-story-high, skylit atrium, in the center of which is a 60-ft-high travertine and granite waterfall sculpture.

The anchor tenant here is **Neiman-Marcus**. Other distinctly superior stores include **Tiffany**, **Gucci** and **Louis Vuitton**. And, in a city which is chock-a-block with bookstores, here is **Rizzoli**, one of my great favorites because of its handsome layout and delightful background music.

Copley Place

Exit from Copley Place through its second hotel, the **Marriott**, and arrive on Huntington Avenue, where, to the left, beckoning about 200 yards away, is the dome of the **Christian Science Mother Church**. The 670-ft-long reflecting pool at the centerpiece of the Christian Science International Headquarters. The pool is not just decorative, it is functional as well: it cools water for the center's air-conditioning system and covers an underground garage. Dazzling flower beds and, beyond that, an avenue of linden trees grace the south side of the pool.

48

Boston after dark

On the other side is a dramatic basilica-like structure, a mixture of Byzantine and Italian Renaissance styles, plus the five-story **Colonnade Building**. Tucked in between these two and engulfed by the basilica is the original Mother Church, a Romanesque affair with a square bell-tower and a rough granite facade. A five-story elliptical **Sunday School** building and a 28-story administrative building complete this magnificent urban ensemble.

Guided tours of both churches start at the entrance to the basilica, which is actually the church annex and which is entered through a grand portico of 10 massive limestone columns. The impressive interior is a lovely column-free affair which seats 5,000 on three levels. The pipe-organ is the largest in the Western Hemisphere. The original Mother Church, 'our prayer in stone', has beautiful stained-glass windows depicting great biblical events. On leaving the church, you can enter the adjacent **Christian Science Publishing Society** building and visit the **Mapparium**, a fascinating walk-through giant stained-glass globe of the world with remarkable acoustic properties.

3. The Museum of Science and the Charles River Basin

A museum and a riverside walk. In summer, the walk can be replaced by a 50-minute launch trip and the time saved used for shopping. The museum is closed on Mondays September to May.

– To the start: MBTA *Green (Lechmere) Line to Science Park Station –*

From the MBTA station it is a short walk to the highly acclaimed **Museum of Science** (9am–5pm with extension on Friday until 9pm and longer summer hours; tel: 723-2500), which is very much a hands-on affair. On display are more than 400 exhibits in the fields of astronomy, energy, industry, and natural history. The museum is also strong in physics and biology. Not to be missed, unless you suffer from motion sickness, is the **Mugar Omni Theater** (tel: 723-2500 for show times), where the world's largest movie projector throws wraparound images onto a 76-ft-high domed screen which surrounds the audience like a cocoon. Shows generally last 45 minutes. Less exhilarating but more cerebral are the 45-minute

The Museum of Science

lecture-demonstrations against a realistic depiction of the night skies and the fun laser light shows that are frequently presented in the **Charles Hayden Planetarium** (tel: 723-2500 for show times).

Climb to the third-floor cafeteria, not so much to refuel as to enjoy the widespread views of the Charles River Basin to the west and, ringing the city to the south, the Blue Hills. The bridge immediately in front, over which the MBTA trains run, is the **Long-fellow**, often referred to as the Salt and Pepper Bridge. The museum shop has a great selection of adult toys.

Turn left on leaving the museum and, at the end of the bridge, turn left again onto Edwin H Land Boulevard, which crosses the

Longfellow Bridge

narrow **Lechmere Canal**. The tables outside the UNO **pizzeria** are a good place to enjoy a drink while watching the fountain play. Close by is the **Cambridgeside Galleria**, a lively shopping mall, whose tenants include Filene's, Sears and upmarket Abercrombie & Fitch. The Galleria also contains a large, bright, airy fast-food court where an international array of foods are served. Seduced by shopping and yet feeling guilty about abandoning your walk around the Charles River Basin? A compromise can be reached by boarding the launch which berths outside the Galleria: it makes a moderately priced 50-minute voyage around the basin.

Return along the canal to the boulevard and turn left past the Sonesta Hotel to reach **Cambridge Parkway** and the river esplanade. To the right are condominiums, some of whose occupants moor their powerboats at the **Charlesgate Yacht Club**, one of four

Cambridgeside Galleria

A Henry Moore statue at MIT

powerboat marinas on the river. After passing under the **Longfellow Bridge** you will be on Memorial Drive, the most delightful part of the Charles River Basin.

Across the river, dominating the skyline, are the John Hancock and Prudential towers. Beyond the highway, to the right, is the MIT campus. Cross the highway and enter the campus's **Great Courtyard (Killian Court)**, which stretches in front of the monumental **Rogers Building** with its pantheon-like dome and broad Ionic portico. A large Henry Moore sculpture in the courtyard is only one of a dozen outstanding pieces of modern sculpture dotted around the campus.

You have now arrived at, and will cross, the **Harvard Bridge**, which is invariably called the MIT **Bridge**. The funny squiggles painted on the sidewalk are the work of MIT students and maintain a tradition inaugurated in 1958 when a Lambda Chi Alpha fraternity novice was required to measure the length of the bridge using himself as a yardstick. The view toward the mouth of the river, with the MIT campus on the left, Back Bay and Beacon Hill with the glistening dome of the State House to the right and, behind that, downtown skyscrapers and the river vibrant with sailing boats and shells, is one of which I never tire.

At the end of the bridge, descend the steps on the left and start your return journey along the Boston side of the river. On this stretch, all Boston turns out for roller-skating, cycling, jog-

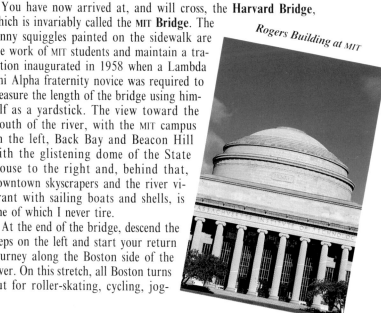

Rogers Building at MIT

Jogging along the Charles River

ging and strolling. In pleasant weather, less energetic sorts sunbathe or feed the ducks. On the right, the idyllic **Storrow Lagoon**, spanned by four small-arched stone bridges, extends for about a mile.

Then comes the **Hatch Shell** and a large bust of **Arthur Fiedler**, who, through his Boston Pops outdoor concerts, brought classical music to the masses. Music still fills the air here in summer. About 300 yards farther along is the clubhouse of **Community Boating**, believed to be the oldest and largest public sailing program in the world. Immediately beyond the club, a stairway leads to the Longfellow Bridge and the Charles Street MBTA station. Trains take you back to Boston or to Cambridge in about 5 minutes.

Afternoon Itineraries

4. Faneuil Hall Market and the Waterfront

An afternoon visit to Faneuil Hall (Quincy) Marketplace, Boston's most popular tourist attraction, and then a stroll to the born-again waterfront and the New England Aquarium.

– To the start: MBTA Green Line (Lechmere) to Government Center –

On leaving the subway station, cross the empty plaza in front of City Hall, descend a flight of steps, cross Congress Street and enter the fun world of **Faneuil Hall Marketplace** or, as it is often called, **Quincy Market**. Boutiques and stalls abound; an infinite number of

Faneuil Hall Marketplace

eating places compete for customers; and scheduled buskers – jugglers, clowns, musicians, magicians – frequently perform. This is the place to pamper yourself by buying that small something you have always wanted to own or to purchase gifts for those back home. The market consists of three long buildings. Near the flower market you can hail a hansom cab for a not inexpensive 20-minute ride. The ground floor of the main building bulges with dozens of food stalls. You might stop for a turkey sandwich at the **Prime Shoppe** or swordfish kebabs at the **Boston & Maine Fish Company**, which also has a raw bar. Wash this down with coffee from the **Coffee Connection** or an exotic alcohol-free Caribbean drink at the **Monkey Bar**. Your selection made, look for a seat at one of the butcher's block tables in the rotunda or sit outside on the benches in the mall.

As you relax over your refreshments, consider the fact that the marketplace was constructed in 1826 and served for almost 150 years as a retail and wholesale distribution center for meat and produce. By the 1970s the area was run-down and due for demolition. Fortunately, recycling became the buzzword and the market was renovated to its former glory, setting a model for the resurgence of urban marketplaces throughout the United States.

East end of the Marketplace

More than 100 retail stores compete for customers in the two lateral buildings, which also contain restaurants. In the **North Market** (No 30) is **Durgin Park** (tel: 227-2038), a Boston institution, where tourists stand in line simply in order to sit at long tables and be insulted by servers who dish up brontosaurus-sized prime ribs. Next to it is the **Marketplace Grill and Oar Bar** (tel: 227-2972), which dishes up tasty new American fare. Both are moderately priced. Two disparate buildings close off the market. At the west end is the 18th-century **Faneuil Hall**, which you might have visited on *Day 1*. At the east end is the **Marketplace Center**, which offers more trendy stores.

Past the freeway beyond the marketplace, you might care to enter **Columbus Park** to relax on a bench in the cobblestone plaza at the water's edge. To the left is the recycled **Commercial Wharf** building, one of several waterfront buildings now occupied by condominiums rather than warehouses. Moored in front are owners' yachts rather than the cargo ships of the past.

Revived, walk through the **Marriott Hotel** – a public right of

The waterfront and condominiums

way – to **Long Wharf**, once the kingpin of Boston's great harbor. The wharf ends in a handsome esplanade, where you can gaze across a harbor busy with scudding sailboats, excursion launches and planes taking off from Logan Airport. Following the blue line painted on the sidewalk, you will arrive at **Central Wharf**, on which stands the **New England Aquarium** (tel: 973-5200), open daily from 9am–5pm or, on some days, even later. Inside, the Giant Ocean Tank ascends for three stories; a ramp encircling it, passes more than 70 wall tanks containing a plethora of fish. Moored alongside the main-building is the **Discovery Theatre**, a floating pavilion whose design is evocative of a Mississippi river steamer. Here dolphins and sea-lions demonstrate how intelligent they are. This being Boston, the shows are educational and are not simply devoted to putting the animals through their paces performing entertaining tricks.

The Aquarium

After a visit to the Aquarium you may have developed a taste for seafood. It's a short walk to the **Boston Harbor Hotel** (tel: 439-7000), a new waterside showplace, where the **Rowes Walk Café** offers irresistible views to go with the food. This is the drop-off point for the **Water Shuttle** to Logan, a pleasant way to leave town, and several dinner cruise ships are moored here as well. A few blocks farther south, and across the Northern Avenue Bridge, is the **Barking Crab** (tel: 426-2722), a citified lobster hut serving New England seafood specialties.

5. Charlestown

Water Shuttle to Charlestown

Charlestown is famous for the Battle of Bunker Hill and its Navy Yard, whose well-known tenant is the USS Constitution.

– To the start: The most enjoyable way to reach the Navy Yard is to take the Blue (Wonderland) Line of the MBTA to Aquarium, and then walk the few yards to the start of Long Wharf, where the MBTA-Navy Yard Water Shuttle departs at frequent intervals –

The 10-minute voyage across Boston Harbor is a delight. The Tobin Bridge, toward which the water shuttle heads, is a major link between Boston and the North Shore. Resisting the temptation to board the free bus to the *Constitution* which meets the water shuttle, walk instead to the foot of the pier and visit the small, intriguing museum of the **Boston Marine Society** (tel: 242-0522), open Monday to Friday 10am–3pm. The main purposes of this society, formed in 1742 by Boston sea captains, were 'to make navigations more safe,' and to start a 'box' – it can be seen and still functions – which provides assistance to distressed members and their families. The society still appoints the Pilot Commissioners who in turn appoint the Boston Harbor pilots.

Turning right on leaving the Marine Society, you'll reach the **National Park Service Visitor Center** (tel: 242-5670; open 10am–4pm in winter, 9am–6pm in summer) and the USS *Constitution*. En route, the octagonal building to the right is the **Muster House**. After passing, to the left, the **Scales House**, the formal entrance to the Navy Yard, you'll pass, again on the right-hand side, the **Commandant's House**.

USS Constitution

The *Constitution* was built in Boston and first sailed from here in 1797 on a shakedown cruise. She was decommissioned after three decades after participating in 42 victorious engagements, including the sinking of the British warship *Guerrière*. During this engagement the *Constitution* earned the sobriquet 'Old Ironsides' when a sailor, on seeing the enemy's cannon balls apparently bouncing off the side, exclaimed: 'Her sides are made of iron!' The rea-

Sailors at the 'Constitution'

son was more mundane: the *Constitution* had been constructed of live oak, which is said to be five times more durable than white oak.

The *Constitution* is the oldest commissioned warship in the world. Derelict in 1830, the ship earned a reprieve when young Oliver Wendell Holmes wrote: 'Ay! pull her tattered ensign down, / Long has it waved on high,' which touched the nation's heartstrings. Then, in 1911, when she was to end life as a target ship, the Massachusetts Society of the Daughters of 1812 intervened. Finally, in the 1920s, Boston schoolchildren contributed their pennies for her restoration. Every July 4, tugs pull her into the harbor for the 'turnaround,' which serves the double purpose of weathering the ship evenly and keeping it in commission.

Boarding the *Constitution*, which is open daily from 9.30am–3.45pm, is no easy matter; long lines are often the order of the day. On board, Navy enlistees in 1812 uniform conduct guided tours and answer questions. If you fail to board the *Constitution*, then you might like to visit the **Constitution Museum** (open 10am–4pm, 5pm or 6pm depending on season; tel: 426-1812) just to the east, where it's possible to experience life below decks. Here you can put your hands on a steering wheel, climb into a hammock or hoist the sail on a moving 'deck' with the sounds of shipboard life all around. Also on show is a walk-through model of keel and ribbing, and *Honor of War*, a continuous audiovisual program that depicts a bloody battle of 1812.

Returning to the Visitor Center and turning left, you'll reach, after 200 yards, the rear of a large, somewhat austere restaurant. Walk around and enter **Barrett's** (tel: 242-9600) where, on the second floor, afternoon refreshments are served. The views of the *Constitution* from the terrace are glo-

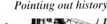

Pointing out history

rious. Another nearby restaurant has earned national accolades: **Olives**, at 10 City Square (tel: 242-1999; dinner only). Its casual cousin, **Figs** (tel: 242-2229), is also appealing. For post-Revolutionary atmosphere, visit the **Warren Tavern** (tel: 241-8142), dating from 1780.

Within walking distance is the **Bunker Hill Monument and**

Charlestown view

Museum (9am–5pm, tel: 242-1843). At the latter an enjoyable 25-minute wrap-around multimedia show, *The Whites of Their Eyes*, offers an excellent introduction to the history of Battle of Bunker Hill. The title refers to Colonel William Prescott's battle order to the American troops not to shoot 'till you see the whites of their eyes.'

On leaving the Bunker Hill pavilion, turn left, walk to the traffic lights, cross the road and pass under the approaches to the Tobin Bridge to Gray Street. From here there is a grand view of your next goal – the Bunker Hill Monument. A right turn at Park Street leads to **Winthrop Square**, which, for a century, was the **Training Field** where Charlestown boys learned the art of war. Cross the square and exit through a gate flanked by bronze tablets commemorating those killed on June 17, 1775. The soaring 220-ft-high **Bunker Hill Monument** is just ahead.

Although the monument honors, it does not mark where the battle took place: that lies about 300 yards to the north. Alongside the monument is a small museum with several exhibits, including an excellent diorama of the battle. Those who feel energetic might wish to climb the 294 stairs to the top, which is open from 9am–4.30pm, but the views are not that rewarding. The bronze figure standing on a pedestal in front of the monument is of Colonel Prescott, the American commander.

Leave Monument Square by the Massachusetts Gate and walk down Monument Avenue to Warren Street, a distance of about 400 yards, where the 93 bus may be boarded for Haymarket and its subway station.

Bunker Hill monument to Colonel Prescott

6. Magnificent Art Collections

An afternoon devoted to the Isabella Stewart Gardner Museum and the Museum of Fine Arts (both closed on Monday).

– To the start: MBTA Green Line-E (Heath) and get off at the Ruggles stop, which is right outside the MFA –

The Museum of Fine Arts (MFA) is generally ranked second only to New York's Metropolitan Museum. Exiting from the subway, walk along Museum Street for a couple of hundred yards to the Fenway, passing en route the MFA (we shall be coming back here later). If you intend to dine at the MFA's **Fine Arts Restaurant**, which offers moderately priced menus themed for changing exhibitions (dinner is served Wednesday to Friday, lunch daily), then this is the time to make a reservation. Now turn left past the Museum School and, in a few giant steps, reach the **Isabella Stewart Gardner Museum** (tel: 566-1401), one of the most magical private museums in the world. It is open Tuesday to Sunday 11am–5pm.

Fenway Court, as the Venetian-style palazzo housing this unique jewel is called, was built in 1902 by Isabella Gardner, an eccentric New Yorker who married Jack Lowell Gardner and became a not-so-proper Bostonian. Legend has it that she drank beer rather than tea, and walked her pet lions in the Back Bay. Her portrait, painted by John Singer Sargent, hangs in Fenway Court, and caused a scandal because of what was then considered a daring décolleté.

Bernard Berenson advised Mrs Gardner on acquisitions, but their presentation and positioning is the result of her inimitable approach. Each room is decorated in a different style, although none is true to any specific period. Mrs Gardner died in 1924 and her will stipulated that the furnishings remain exactly as she arranged them; otherwise the building and its contents were to be sold and

The Gardner Museum

the proceeds given to Harvard University. Were it not for this legal embalment a good part of her collection could be consigned to the storeroom. Nobody, however, would do that to her Giotto or Piero della Francesca; or her Titian, easily the most beautiful in America, which is given added resonance by Mrs Gardner's lovely setting.

Even those impervious to Dutch baroque and Italian Renaissance masterpieces, to Titians and Rembrandts, Whistlers and Sargents, Matisses and Manets, stained glass and textiles, are sure to delight in the central courtyard, many of whose elements were imported from Venice and which, throughout the year, is ablaze with flowers. To sit here, away from the madding crowd, is nothing less than sheer bliss. So, too, are chamber music concerts in the subdued tapestry room on the second floor. These are held from September to May on Saturdays and Sunday at 1.30pm.

Time for afternoon tea. At the Gardner, it is a joy to take a tray into the outdoor garden. However, I think it is preferable to make for the **Museum of Fine Arts** and enjoy afternoon tea in the delightful first-floor **Galleria Café**. An alternative is the self-service cafeteria in the MFA's basement, from where you may carry trays into the central courtyard. Both stay open into the evening on Wednesday to Friday.

Refreshed, you're ready to tackle the galleries of the MFA (tel: 267-9300), which show the works of eight departments: Asiatic, which includes Chinese, Japanese, Korean, Indian and Islamic Art; Egyptian Art; Classical Art; European decorative arts and sculpture; American decorative arts and sculpture; paintings, prints, drawings and photographs; textiles and costumes; and 20th century art. In addition, a temporary exhibition is invariably on display in the West Wing.

The Asiatic and Egyptian departments have superb collections. Indeed, the Japanese collection is unrivaled in the world and the assembly of

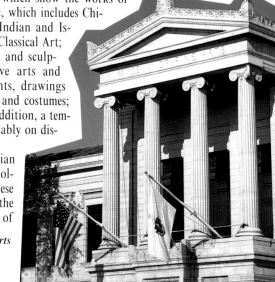

Museum of Fine Arts

'Boston Common at Twilight' by F C Hassam

Egyptian artifacts is the most complete outside Cairo. The American collection contains not only canvases but more than enough Americana, including Paul Revere silver, to satisfy all the Daughters of the American Revolution.

The museum (10am–5pm, also some evenings, but closed Monday (see *Option 7 below*). Before leaving, be sure to visit the MFA's shop. Outside the building turn right to visit, especially in the spring, the fragrant **Japanese Garden**.

Evening Itineraries

7. A Museum Evening

Most Boston museums operate late opening hours at least one evening a week.

The **Museum of Fine Arts** (tel: 267-9300: MBTA Green Line-E) is open on Wednesday, Thursday and Friday until 9pm. The whole musuem is open on Wenedsay, but on Thursday and Friday, only the West Wing opens. The West Wing features temporary exhibitions and special shows and houses the excellent, well-stocked shop.

On all three evenings the Fine Arts Restaurant is open until 8.30pm (reservations recommended); the Galleria Café, which serves light meals, is open until 9.30pm, and the self-service cafeteria, from where trays can be carried into the central open courtyard, is open until 8pm.

After enjoying the art, you can hop on the Green Line-E (Lechmere) to Science Park and visit the **Mugar Omni Theater** in the **Museum of Science**. Late shows are held on Friday and Saturday at 10pm and on Sunday at 9pm, but it is advisable to telephone (723-2500) to confirm times.

On these nights and on other evenings (again, telephone to confirm times), exciting laser shows are presented in the museumof Science's **Planetarium**. Seating for all these shows is limited, so do

Museum of Science

not arrive at the last moment. The **Exhibit Halls** in the museum remain open on Friday until 9pm.

On Wednesday and Thursday during the summer the **New England Aquarium** (MBTA Blue Line to Aquarium) is open until 8pm. For the remainder of the year, only Thursday is a late night (tel: 973-5200).

'There she blows!' A chance to spot a latter-day Moby Dick and an adventurous way to spend a marine/aquatic evening is to make for **Long Wharf** (MBTA Blue Line to Aquarium) and board one of the whale-watching boats which depart on some evenings at 5.30pm for a 4-hour cruise. To check that evening cruises are still operating, contact **Boston Harbor Cruises**; tel: 227-4321. (Five-hour cruises also operate from 9.30am.)

For a brief description of the contents of the Museum of Fine Arts see *Pick & Mix Option 6*, page 58; for that of the Museum of Science see *Pick & Mix Option 3*, page 49; and for that of the New England Aquarium see *Pick & Mix Option 4*, page 52.

'West Church, Boston' by Maurice Prendergast

8. A Sporting Evening

Even if you are not a sports fan, an evening at Fenway Park or at the Boston Garden offers an enjoyable insight into how enthusiastic Bostonians can be over the Red Sox (baseball), the Celtics (basketball) and the Bruins (ice hockey).

– To reach Fenway Park board the MBTA Green Line (B,C, or D) and get off at Kenmore Square, which is a 10-minute walk from the stadium. You can travel directly to the Garden, which is at North Station, by taking the Green or Orange Line of the MBTA –

The **Red Sox** is one of America's favorite baseball teams, and an evening at **Fenway Park** (tel: 267-1770) provides an opportunity to enjoy the smallest major league park and one of the last to retain natural grass. About 50 night games, the majority starting at 7.35pm, are played during a season (start of April until early October, later if the Sox are involved in the play-offs).

Before and after the game, join the regulars for a beer at **Copperfields**, **Who's On First** or the **Cask 'n' Flagon**, all of which are just outside Fenway Park. The last of these serves hearty basic American food, but unless you arrive before 6pm there will be a long line. More upmarket is the **Boston Beer Works**, 61 Brooklyn Avenue (tel:536-2337), a microbrewery offering more adventurous regional cuisine. Landsdowne Street, just around the corner, is packed with dance clubs if you'd like a post-game workout.

The basketball season, during which the **Celtics** play more than 30 evening home games, spans November through April, while the hockey season, during which a similar number of night home games are played by the **Bruins**, begins in October and ends in early April. (These seasons are extended if the teams make the play-offs.) Both teams play at **Boston Garden** (tel: 931 2000); a brand new stadium is in the planning stages. Game time for basketball is 7.30pm while hockey is either 7.05pm or 7.35pm.

After a Garden game, cross the road, and to the right at 138 Portland Street is the **Commonwealth Brewing Company** (tel:

The Bruins in Boston Garden

Starting young

523-8383), which is a good place to knock back a couple of English-style ales, stouts or bitters among glistening copper kettles and pipes. An inexpensive light food menu accompanies the drinks.

Tickets, which are are hard to secure and should be booked in advance (preferably before you even arrive in Boston) can be purchased at Bostix, Faneuil Hall Marketplace (tel: 723-5181) Tuesday to Saturday 10am–6pm, until 4pm on Sunday, closed Monday, or from Bostix on Copley Square, daily 10–6pm. Alternatively try the Out of Town Ticket Agency (tel: 247 2300) in the concourse of the subway at Harvard Square, which is open 9am–6pm; 5.30pm on Saturday; closed Sunday.

9. An Evening Around Harvard Square

Although Harvard Square is student-oriented, the spots mentioned in this evening's entertainment are mainly frequented by the mid-30s and older crowd and a decent dress standard is enforced at several. Reservations are required.

– To the start: MBTA Red Line to Harvard Square or bus route 1 along Massachusetts Avenue to Harvard Square –

Begin the evening with a drink at the **Casablanca** (40 Brattle Street, tel: 876-0999), under whirling ceiling fans and the approving gaze of Humphrey and Ingrid. Large wicker love-seats enhance the ambience. From here, make your way through the square to Harvard's **Hasty Pudding Club** (10 Holyoke Street), renowned worldwide for its Man and Woman of the Year awards. Before reaching the Hasty Pudding, you might stop off at one of the outdoor chess tables at **Au Bon Pain** in the very heart of the square and pit your skills against the locals who challenge all comers.

Casablanca mural

Up the stairs of the Pudding Club is a restaurant called, not surprisingly, **Upstairs at the Pudding** (tel: 864-1933), a long-established dining room which serves North Italian and European cuisine in elegant surroundings, with an unexpected outdoor patio. Dinner complete, wander back through the square to the **Charles Hotel** at the corner of **Eliot** and **Bennett streets**, passing en route a seemingly endless number of street musicians, magicians and jugglers. Some are extremely talented: others, at best, are mediocre. Not so the performers at the **Regattabar** at the Charles. This spacious, elegant club has long established itself as *the* place for jazz in New England, and the George Shearing Duo, the Four Freshmen, Herbie Hancock and Herbie Mann have all played here. Aficionados from New York are known to drive up for showtime which, on Tuesday and Wednesday is 9pm and on Thursday to Saturday 9pm and 11pm, and then return home

Upstairs at the Pudding

again. Reservations (tel: 876-7777) are essential, and, if you're still hungry, the hors d'oeuvres are great.

If you long for more jazz, then grab a cab to **Scullers Jazz Club** (tel: 783-0090) at the **Guest Quarters Suite Hotel**, which is on the Boston (actually the Brighton) side of the Charles River, about a mile from the square. The best of 'the blue notes' fill the air here on Thursday through Saturday: showtime is at 8pm and 10pm.

If jazz is not your scene, then folk music and comedy clubs – dress at these is less formal and the crowd younger – can be enjoyed in the heart of the square. **Passim** (tel: 492-7679), a below-street-level survivor from the early '70s which gave many greats their first chance and on which much of Boston's reputation as a folk mecca rests, is situated at the corner of Church and Palmer streets. By day it's a gift shop and café, but come evening it's transformed into a setting for folk music. Showtimes vary.

Buskers in Harvard Square

Finally, on the south side of the square, at 30 John F Kennedy Avenue is **Catch a Rising Star** (tel: 661-9877), a club, part of a national chain, where comedy rules the stage for seven nights a week. Nationally acclaimed acts appear from Tuesday to Saturday, while local talent gets its opportunity on Sunday and Monday. There are late shows on Friday and Saturday: the humor is decidedly local.

10. A Night on the Town

Boston is not known for its nightlife, but the opportunity exists, especially on weekends, to enjoy unusual theater and comedy clubs. The places mentioned here are all close to one another; reservations are essential at most.

– To the start: MBTA Green Line (B,C,D,E) to Arlington Street –

Start the evening with pre-dinner drinks at either the **Ritz-Carlton** (15 Arlington Street; tel: 536-5700) or **Biba** (272 Boylston Street, tel: 426-7878). Each has a bar overlooking the Public Garden. At the former, which tends to attract old money, order from their unique martini menu which lists and describes 13 of these cocktails. Although Biba, which is frequented by a more adventurous clientele, does not serve such a variety of martinis, spirits are much higher and decibels greater.

Each place also has an upstairs restaurant overlooking the garden. Dinner at Biba, invariably listed among Boston's top three restaurants, is fairly expensive and accompanied by razzamatazz and much noise. The setting at the Ritz, with white linen and crystal chandeliers, is much more sedate and the cuisine is French; the pricees are about as high as Boston goes. If you must ask the cost then you probably cannot afford it. A more moderately priced meal can be enjoyed in the **Ritz Café**, which, however, does not enjoy a view of the Public Garden.

Dining on a completely different level and in a time-warp can be experienced at **Jacob Wirth** (31 Stuart Street, tel: 338-8586), where all the furniture and fittings are from 1868. The restaurant is old enough and distinguished enough to be on the National Register of Historic Places. Meals here are inexpensive. Gourmands might wish to order the German dinner of pigs' trotters, roast

pork, ribs and *sauerkraut* or cabbage, and wash it down with a heady, specially brewed beer.

Toward the end of the week (Wednesday through Saturday) there is a choice of off-beat theater and comedy clubs. (At the beginning of the week, their programs start too early to permit a leisurely dinner.) All these entertainments are located within a 10-minute walk of the restaurants just mentioned.

The Charles Playhouse (74–78 Warrenton Street, tel: 426-6912), which is on the National Register of Historic Places, is the theater district's oldest playhouse and today has two stages running a mix of off-Broadway-style musicals and cabaret acts; a third stage in the same complex is occupied by the **Comedy Connection** (tel: 391-0022).

Up the road from the Charles is **Nick's Comedy Stop** at 100 Warrenton Street (tel: 482-0930). Out-of-towners, especially those from abroad, may find it difficult to understand some of the local context to the humor.

Several large, historic theaters are also located nearby. The Colonial (tel: 426-9366), **Shubert** (tel: 426-4520) and **Wilbur** (tel: 423-4008) theaters book popular traveling dramas and musicals. The **Emerson Majestic Theatre** (tel: 824-8000), now operated by Emerson College, offers a more affordably-priced, often eclectic alternative to mainstream theater.

The 3,800-seat **Wang Center for the Performing Arts** (tel: 482-9393) hosts major events, such as the Boston Ballet's invariably sold-out *Nutcracker*, which is the most popular production in the world.

Sunset on the Charles River

EXCURS

11. Concord and Lexington

A full day's visit to historical Lexington and Concord. This itinerary can be made by public transportation, but a car is preferable. Most sites are closed on Sunday morning and from November until mid-April. Many places visited on this itinerary insist on guided tours and visitors may be required to wait before sightseeing begins. These guided tours usually last about 40 minutes.

– To the start: Drive from Boston to Lexington on Route 2 west, a distance of 12 miles. Alternatively, board the Red Line of the MBTA to Alewife and then Bus 62 (Bedford) or 76 (Hanscom Field) to Lexington center. After exploring, take a taxi for the 8 miles to Concord and return from there to Boston's North Station by commuter train: about 40 minutes –

Arriving at Battle Green, a triangular park in the heart of **Lexington**, you will be greeted by the **Minuteman Statue,** which honors those Minutemen who responded to Captain Parker's exhortation on April 19, 1775: 'Stand your ground, don't fire unless fired upon, but if they mean to have a war, let it begin here!' And so began the American Revolution.

Minuteman Statue

To the right (east) of the green is **Buck-man Tavern**, a clapboard building which has been restored to its original late 17th-century condition. After the battle, the Minutemen who had been wounded were carried into this tavern for medical attention. As you explore the tavern (daily; tel: 861-0928), observe the bullet holes in the door from the battle, muskets and cooking equipment used at the time, and the original 17th-century furniture.

From here, a short stroll north brings you to the **Hancock-Clarke House** (summer only), where, on the evening of April 18, 1771, John Hancock and Samuel Adams were roused from their slumbers and warned of the coming of the British by Paul Revere. The house (daily; tel: 862-5598), furnished in colonial style, was built in 1738 and is now a museum of the Revolution.

Before setting off for Concord, have coffee at the **Coffee Connection** at 1729 Massachusetts Avenue. Then call for a taxi (A-1 Taxi of Lexington, tel: 863-2626, or drive along **Route 2A**.

Down the lazy river

This follows, more or less, **Battle Road,** along which the British marched, harried by the Minutemen. 'How the farmers gave them ball for ball / From behind each fence and farm-yard wall.'

After about 8 miles you'll see **The Wayside** (May to end September, Monday to Thursday; tel: 508-369-6975) on the right, the first of the literary homes to which **Concord** owes much of its fame. The Alcotts and then Nathaniel Hawthorne lived here. Explore the tower study where Hawthorne attempted to write, eventually turning in despair to travel writing and saying he would be happy if the house burned down. It did not and was later occupied by Margaret Sidney, author of the *Five Little Peppers* books.

Pint-size colonial

Delightful **Orchard House** (tel: 508-369-4118), just along the road, is where the Alcott family lived from 1858 to 1877 and where Louisa wrote her classic novel *Little Women,* and her father, Bronson, founded his school of philosophy.

Another hop, skip and a jump to the junction of Lexington Road and the Cambridge Turnpike leads to the splendid **Concord Antiquarian Museum** (tel: 508-369-9069), where you can tour 17 rooms of antiques spanning the 17th to 19th centuries. Visitors who are not skeptics will enjoy being shown one of the two lanterns which were hung in the Old North Church to signal that the redcoats were leaving for Concord and Lexington. Here, too, is Emerson's study, which, apart from one round table, was transferred in its entirety from the wooden **Emerson House** across the road because of fear of fire, and the Thoreau Room containing the bed in which the great man slept in his Walden hut. Emerson enthusiasts will wish to visit his home (tel: 508-369-2236; closed in winter), in which all the furnishings – other than those in the study – are original and where he wrote his essays.

And so to **Monument Square** in the center of Concord, at the far side of which stands, as it has done for years, **The Colonial Inn** (tel: 508-369-9200), a fine place for a traditional New England lunch or a lighter menu. On leaving the inn, stroll along Bedford Street (Route 62) to **Sleepy Hollow Cemetery**. In an idyllic setting in the northeast corner lies **Authors' Ridge**, the final resting place of Hawthorne, the Alcotts, Emerson and Thoreau. Then drive north for about a mile on Monument Street.

Old North Bridge

Cross the main road and stroll to the **Old North Bridge**, which inspired the renowned ode 'The rude bridge that spanned the Flood.' Here, Major John Buttrick appealed to the Minutemen: 'Fire, fellow soldiers, for God's sake, fire!' The 'genuine look' antique bridge spans the **Concord River**; on the other side is the famous **Minuteman Statue**, rifle in one hand, in the other a ploughshare. Ralph Waldo Emerson's immortal words, 'the shot heard 'round the world' are inscribed on the plinth. The **North Bridge Visitor Center** is open daily from 8.30am–6pm. Here are dioramas and gardens overlooking the river.

Before crossing the main road to the parking lot, turn right to the clapboard **Old Manse** (tel: 508-369-3909, closed Tuesday), built in 1770 and first occupied by the Reverend William Emerson, who watched the battle for the bridge from here. A tour of the house, which was later occupied by Ralph Waldo Emerson and then Haw-thorne, is enjoyable.

Walden Pond

And so to the last stop on this day tour, **Walden Pond**, best reached by car. The pond is famous for its association with Henry David Thoreau. However, none of the ambiance immortalized by Thoreau when he wrote 'the mass of men who lead quiet lives of desperation' is evident in the summer when the pond becomes the local swimming hole.

The 1½-mile circumambulation of the pond is a delight. Not far from the north end, the walk passes the site of Thoreau's hut.

Shopping

Chic and funky, antique and ethnic, bargain-basement and rarefied gentility: it's all to be found when shopping in Boston. Most stores open between 9am and 10am and close at 6pm or 7pm, although some, especially at Faneuil Hall, stay open later; on Sundays most do not open their doors until noon.

Childhood magic at FAO Schwartz

Faneuil Hall Marketplace contains more than 150 shops and restaurants, attracting over a million visitors each month. The North and South Markets are bursting with boutiques and national name stores, as is the newer Marketplace Center with its soaring steel, glass and neon canopy. The Bull Market has colorful carts from which handmade crafts and souvenirs are sold.

Downtown Crossing is a brick pedestrian zone, the heart of which is the intersection of Washington and Winter streets, where souvenirs and jewelry are sold from carts. A number of well-established jewelry shops – **DePrisco**, **De Scenza Diamonds**, **The E B Horn Company** – can also be found here. Dominating a score of small stores is **Filene's Basement**, where everyone is hoping to find a sensational bargain. An $800 Brooks Brothers suit may, for example, go on sale at $400; if unsold after 14 days, it's reduced to $200; after 21 days, $100; after 28 days, $50. After that, if still ungrabbed, it goes to charity. Fun shopping? Sometimes it's a riot!

Downtown Crossing is also home to **Jordan Marsh**, the largest department store in New England, plus what is said to be the world's largest **Woolworth's**.

Faneuil Hall Marketplace

Back Bay (see *Pick & Mix Option 1*), which includes 8-block-long stretches of **Newbury** and **Boylston streets**, is Boston's premier shopping area. The former is lined with chic boutiques and sidewalk cafés. Beyond Fairfield Street chic is replaced by funk, although oases of the former remain. Boylston Street lacks the charm of Newbury yet that part close to the Public Garden has enough upmarket stores to strain the most opulent bank balances.

A relatively new shoppers' delight is **Copley Place** (*Pick & Mix Option 2*), an elegant and glitzy building at the southeast corner of **Copley Square**. The tone of the lower floor is set by classy **Neiman-Marcus**, while the upper floor is devoted to less expensive shops selling mainly clothes.

And so to **Cambridge**. The area in and around **Harvard Square** is chock-a-block with stores, most of which have a youthful appeal. Some stores are gathered in mini-malls such as **The Garage** and the **Galleria**, both on John F Kennedy Street; **Holyoke Center,** off Massachusetts Avenue; and **The Shops at Charles Place** in the hotel complex at Bennett and Eliot streets. Stores are not restricted to Harvard Square but extend eastwards and northwards along Massachusetts Avenue to Central Square and Porter Square respectively, with quality falling along with the price of the rents.

Newbury Street in Back Bay

Since Harvard has the largest university library in the world, it is hardly surprising that Cambridge claims to have the greatest concentration of bookshops in the nation. Most are in and around Harvard Square and some remain open until midnight. They include **Grolier's**, the nation's only all-poetry bookshop; **Revolution Books**, which is devoted to books on revolutionary politics; and **Seven Stars**, which sells New Age books and incense.

Finally, over in **East Cambridge** (get off at Kendall Square on the Green Line) is the handsome **Cambridgeside Galleria** (see *Pick & Mix Option 3*).

Bargains at Filene's Basement

Eating

Many people claim that Boston has the best seafood in the nation. Specialties include clam chowder (made without adding tomatoes); scrod (not a separate species of fish but small, tender haddock or cod); and steamers (clams served with broth and butter). Baked beans, once synonymous with Boston, and Boston brown bread are no longer that popular and may be rather difficult to find. In the late 1980s a renaissance of Boston cuisine occurred, spearheaded by a few imaginative chefs like Jasper White of Jasper's, Michela Larson of Rialto and Chris Schlesinger of the East Coast Grill. Contemporary New England cuisine was born and made its impact on the American scene.

Salad days

As time has passed the dress code at restaurants has become less formal, although a few bastions remain. Traditionally, Bostonians are not late diners and restaurants are fairly busy by 7pm. The city's culinary fame is generally agreed to reside at the high end of the price range with few mid-range restaurants.

A rough guide to prices for a 3-course dinner excluding beverages, tax and tip: $ = under $15; $$ = $15–$28; $$$ = $28–$40; $$$$ = over $40.

Many restaurants not listed on the following pages have been included in the previous itineraries.

Frozen temptation

Seafood

LEGAL SEA FOODS
35 Columbus Avenue
Tel: 426-4444 and
Copley Place
Tel: 266-7775
Former small fish store now has big reputation. No reservations. Lines can be long. **$$–$$$**

SKIPJACKS
500 Boylston Street
Tel: 536-3500, and
2 Brooklyn Place
Tel: 232-8887
Generous portions, inventive presentations and a stylish setting. **$$**

TURNER FISHERIES
Westin Hotel, Copley Place
Tel: 424-7425
On a par with Legal Seafoods, but more expensive. **$$$**

American

BAY TOWER ROOM
60 State Street
Tel: 723-1666
Dine on the 33rd floor for the views, seen from all tables, of the waterfront and beyond, rather than for the contemporary cuisine. Dinner only. Jacket and tie. Reservations advised. **$$$$**

BLUE DINER
150 Kneeland Street
Tel: 338-4639
Blueplate specials served in genuine restored diner from 1947. Vintage rock on the juke box and music selector at each booth. **$–$$**

GRILL-23 & BAR
161 Berkeley Street
Tel: 542-2255
Clubby-type upmarket steakhouse with high noise level. Excellent wines. **$$$$**

HAMERSLEY'S BISTRO
539 Tremont Street
Tel: 267-6068
An intimate charmer in the South End, where friendly service accompanies exciting and delightful contemporary New England cuisine. Reservations essential. $$$–$$$$

ROWES WHARF RESTAURANT
Boston Harbour Hotel
70 Rowes Wharf
Tel: 439-3995
This restaurant specialises in exquisite New American cuisine, with the added advantage of views over Bustling Boston harbor. $$$$

Southern

EAST COAST GRILL
1271 Cambridge Street
Tel: 491-6568
Crowded shop-restaurant with no ambience and many decibels which serves superb southern food. No reservations required. $$$

MAGNOLIA'S
1193 Cambridge Street
Tel: 576-1971
Cajun at its best. Small menu written on blackboard in snug dining room. No reservations. $$$

Continental

LOCKE-OBER CAFÉ
3 Winter Place
Tel: 542-1340
This 'Bastion of Brahmins' with a gentlemen's club atmosphere opened a century ago. Some waiters seem to have been there ever since. Visitors die for Lobster Savannah and Baked Alaska (order ahead). Outstanding wine list. Jacket and tie; reservations. If this is your scene, this is a 'must.' $$$$

International

SONSIE
327 Newbury Street
Tel: 351-2500
The youthful end of Newbury Street has an appropriately trendsetting – and ultra-chic – café. $$$

French

AUJOURD'HUI
200 Boylston Street
Tel: 451-1392
Truly superb contemporary dishes, excellent wines in an opulent dining room overlooking the Public Garden. Jacket. $$$$

Italian

Boston has numerous Italian restaurants, many of them situated in 'Little Italy' (the North End).

CIAO BELLA
240A Newbury Street
Tel: 536-2626
Upscale spot for the trendy crowd serving excellent Italian cuisine. Outdoor dining. $$

RIALTO
Charles Hotel
Harvard Square
Tel: 661-5050
Outstanding cuisine combined with elegant surroundings make this Boston's *numero uno* Italian restaurant. It is particularly noted for its fabulous wine list, and make a good choice for a special occasion. $$$$

RISTORANTE TOSCANO
41 Charles Street
Tel: 723-4090
More wonderful Italian food, this time in an elegant but very convival Florentine-style trattoria. $$$–$$$$

ROCCO'S
5 Charles Street South
Tel: 723-6800
North Italian-style restaurant, specialising in a hearty, rustic cuisine, served in an eccentric, citified setting. $$$$

German

JACOB WIRTH
31 Stuart Street.
Tel: 338-8586
Jacob Wirth is a true time-warp in the theater district and it is worth a visit for this reason alone. Since 1868 first-rate *wurst*, *sauerkraut* and specially brewed beer have attracted visitors to this institution with a sawdust floor. On the National Historic Register. $–$$

Chinese

NEW HOUSE OF TOY
16 Hudson Street
Tel: 426-5587
Specializes in Cantonese cuisine. Offers wonderful choice of dishes, including some 60 different varieties of *dim sum*. $$

CARL'S PAGODA
23 Tyler Street
Tel: 357-9837
Unpretentious, serving great Cantonese food. Bring your own bottle. No reservations. $$

Japanese

GYUHAMA
827 Boylston Street
Tel: 437-0188
A popular Back Bay restaurant, especially for *sushi*. $$

TATSUKICHI
189 State Street
Tel: 720-2468
Consistently one of the best Japanese restaurants. Stick to the ground floor; superb raw fish and interesting house specials. Reservations suggested. $$$

Thai

BANGKOK CUISINE
177A Massachusetts Avenue
Tel: 262-5377
The oldest of Boston's Thai restaurants, this small shop-restaurant with somewhat garish decor is usually given

Luxury dining at Boston Harbor Hotel

the nod as the leading Thai in town. No reservations. **$$**

THAI DISH
259 Newbury Street
Tel: 437-9611 and
Subtly spiced Thai food combines with low-key decor. Outdoor dining in summer. **$$**

THE KING AND I
145 Charles Street
Tel: 227-3320
The sister restaurant to the Thai Dish.

Indian

KEBAB-N-CURRY
30 Massachusetts Avenue
Tel: 536-9835
Pleasant, intimate ambience with helpful waiters keen to advise. Especially good tandooris. **$$**

INDIAN PAVILION
17 Central Square, Cambridge
Tel: 547-7463
A hole-in-the-wall restaurant popular with both Indians and students. Recommended for the tandooris, but other dishes also good. **$$**

Pizza

BERTUCCI'S
21 Brattle Street
Harvard Square
Tel: 864-4748 and
22 Merchant's Row
Faneuil Hall Marketplace
Tel: 227-7889 and other locations
Inexpensive chain, with decent house wine. **$**

Nightlife

Because of tradition and its many schools, Boston is the most musical city in the nation, considering its size. Internationally renowned is the Boston Symphony Orchestra, with concerts from November to May. Long lines form early (three hours in advance) for discounted same-day, one-per-customer seats available Tuesday, Thursday and Friday.

The Boston Philharmonic Orchestra, whom some prefer even to Symphony, mounts a half dozen concerts in the course of the winter. A wide range of concerts, generally free, is offered at the New England Conservatory of Music, and a multitude of excellent modern (jazz, etc) musical events, free or at very reasonable prices, can be enjoyed at the Berklee Performance Center. Chamber music and choral groups abound. In winter, Saturday and Sunday afternoon chamber music concerts at the Gardner Museum are especially enjoyable.

Theater in Boston runs the gamut from Broadway shows to college productions by way of repertory and experimental theater. Boston has also long been a tryout town for pre-Broadway productions. Among the more distinguished local companies is the American Repertory Theatre which presents new American plays and modern interpretations of the classics at Harvard's Loeb Drama Center in Cambridge.

The city's premier dance company, which performs at the Wang Center, is the Boston Ballet whose repertory includes classical and modern works. Other noteworthy dance events are held in various venues by the Dance Umbrella, a non-profit organization.

Stand-up comedy too

Subject to availability, half-price tickets on the day of performances can be purchased at the Bostix booth at Faneuil Hall Marketplace and at a kiosk in Copley Square: call 723-5181 for recorded information.

Dancing can be enjoyed at the Roxy and the Zanzibar, two clubs downtown that demand a decent dress standard and where you will not feel out of place if you are over 30. The younger crowd make their way to the discos, which are vast and which are situated around and beyond Kenmore Square. They stay open until 2am.

The Thursday *Globe* and the weekly *Phoenix* carry complete entertainment listings for the week. Major venues not listed here can be found in the appropriate evening itinerary.

Music

BERKLEE PERFORMANCE CENTER
136 Massachusetts Avenue
Tel: 266-7455

JORDAN HALL (NEC)
30 Gainsborough Street
Tel: 536-2412

SYMPHONY HALL
301 Massachusetts Avenue
Tel: 266-1492

THE WANG CENTER FOR THE PERFORMING ARTS
270 Tremont Street
Tel: 482-9393

Jazz

BAY TOWER ROOM
60 State Street
Tel:723-1666

PLAZA BAR
Copley Plaza Hotel
138 St James Avenue
Copley Square
Tel: 267-5300

ZACHARY'S BAR:
Colonnade Hotel
120 Huntingdon Avenue
Tel: 424-7000

Theater

BOSTON UNIVERSITY THEATRE
264 Huntington Avenue
Tel: 266-3913

CHARLES PLAYHOUSE
74 Warrenton Street
Tel: 426-5225

EMERSON MAJESTIC THEATER
219 Tremont Street
Tel: 824-8000

LOEB DRAMA CENTER
64 Brattle Street, Cambridge
Tel: 547-8300

Music is everywhere in Boston

Emerson Majestic Theater

SHUBERT THEATRE
265 Tremont Street
Tel: 426-4520

WILBUR THEATRE
246 Tremont Street
Tel: 423-4008

Pubs and Clubs

BLACK ROSE
160 State Street
Tel: 742-2286
Irish pub with live music nightly.

BULL & FINCH
84 Beacon Street
Tel: 227-9605
The Bull & Finch pub is Boston's third most popular attraction. Expect long lines at this fun place, which has dancing from Thursday to Saturday.

College chorus line

HOULIHAN'S
Faneuil Hall Marketplace
60 State Street
Tel: 367-6377
Informal but upscale bar and burger restaurant with nightly dancing.

PURPLE SHAMROCK
1 Union Street
Tel: 227-2060
Irish pub with live music nightly.

Gay Scene

For listings check, *Bay Windows*, a gay paper, or 'One in Ten' a supplement of the *Boston Phoenix*.

CHAPS
31 Huntington Street
Tel: 266-7778
A long-standing gay bar.

CLUB CAFÉ
209 Columbus Avenue
Tel: 536-0966
Mainly, but not exclusively, gay clientèle. Live music nightly and cabaret shows.

NAPOLEON CLUB
52 Piedmont Street
Tel: 338-7547
Oldest gay club in the nation with nightly piano bar. Aging patrons will feel at ease in the wrinkle room.

PARADISE CAFÉ
180 Massachusetts Avenue
Cambridge
Tel: 864-4130
A low-key men's bar near MIT

1270 CLUB
1270 Boylston Street
Tel: 437-1257
Large gay disco on three floors with a basement piano bar and dancing on the two upper levels. Outdoor roof deck opens at lunchtime in summer.

Calendar of Special Events

A list of some of the celebrations which will appeal to visitors. Public holidays are marked with an asterisk.

JANUARY

New Year's Day* (1st).
Martin Luther King Day*
Chinese New Year (end of January or early February): celebrated in traditional style in Chinatown.

FEBRUARY

Boston Festival (mid-Feb): lasting one month, with a Valentine's celebration, followed by a food festival with ice sculptures and various activities.
Washington's Birthday* (third Monday): a ceremony is held at Washington's statue in Public Garden.

MARCH

Boston Massacre and Crispus Attucks Day (5th): parade sets off from the massacre site to City Hall Plaza.

Columbus Day

New England Spring Flower Show (middle of month): the oldest continuing flower exhibition in the nation, it lasts for seven days.
St Patrick's Day Parade (Sunday before March 17): held in South Boston.

APRIL

Easter Sunday*: join the throngs who walk to the Common in their best finery.
Eve of Patriots' Day (third Sunday): lantern service at Old North Church.
Patriots' Day* (third Monday): many celebrations take place, especially in Concord and Lexington.
Boston Marathon (third Monday): the renowned annual joggers' race.

MAY

Boston Pops (mid-May): commencement of a six-week season at Symphony Hall.
Memorial Day* (last Monday in May): parade from Copley Square ending in a ceremony at Fenway Rose Garden.

Festival on the Common

JUNE

Ancient & Honorable Artillery Company Parade (first Monday): the nation's third oldest standing military organization celebrates.
Back Bay Street Fair (first Saturday): features food, drink, arts and crafts and great live music.
Bunker Hill Day (Sunday before the 17th): features a re-enactment of the Battle of Bunker Hill, and parades in Charlestown.

JULY

Boston Pops: free concerts month-long in the Hatch Memorial Shell.
Independence Day* (4th): reading of Declaration of Independence at the Old State House.
Harborfest (4th): turnaround of the *USS Constitution* and fireworks.
Chowderfest (early in month).
Religious processions and feasts (most weekends in July and August): brass bands and lots of food in the mostly Italian North End.

AUGUST

August Moon Festival (movable): prancing lions and dragons and lots of exotic foods in Chinatown.

SEPTEMBER

Labor Day* (first Monday).
Back Bay Street Dance (second Saturday).
Cambridge River Festival (mid-Sept): music and bazaar on Memorial Drive.
Charles Street Fair (Sunday late in month): traditional fall celebration on Beacon Hill's main shopping street.

OCTOBER

Columbus Day*: parade in East Boston or the North End.
Head of the Charles Regatta (second-to-last Sunday): largest one-day crew race in the world.

The Boston Marathon

NOVEMBER

Veterans Day*: parade starts on Commonwealth Avenue in Back Bay.
Thanksgiving* (fourth Thursday).

DECEMBER

Re-enactment of the Boston Tea Party (16th): at Tea Party Museum.
Carol Singing (24th): Louisburg Square.
First Night (31st): Starts in the afternoon in the Back Bay and continues well into the following year...

83

Unless a separate exchange code is shown, all telephone numbers are for Boston (US area dialing code 617). 1-800 numbers are toll-free if dialed from the US.

GETTING THERE

By Air

Logan Airport has five terminals (A–E). Domestic and international flights of the same airline do not necessarily

The city logo

use the same terminal. Free service between the terminals, including an Airport Handicapped Van, is provided daily 7am–11pm (tel: 561-1769).

Currency may be exchanged at Bay Bank and at Shawmut Bank at Terminal E. Telegrams may be sent from Western Union at Terminal B. Rental

lockers are available at all terminals except D. Hotel reservations can be made at the lower levels of Terminals C and E. Other terminals have direct telephone lines. The nearest hotel is the Logan Airport Hilton.

Logan, 3 miles from downtown Boston, is closer to town than any other major airport in the nation: this refers to distance and not to time. Traffic jams at the two tunnels under the harbor to connect the airport and city are eternal. For up-to-date information on airport traffic conditions call Massport's Ground Transportation Hotline (1-800-235-6426), Monday to Friday, 9am–5pm.

The MBTA Blue Line from Airport Station is the fastest way to downtown (about 10 minutes) and to many other places as well. Free shuttle buses run between all the airport terminals and the subway station.

Cabs can be hired outside each terminal. Fares should average under $20, including tip, providing there are no major traffic jams. Airways Transportation buses (tel: 267-2981) leave all terminals every half hour until 10pm (6pm on Saturday) for downtown and Back Bay hotels.

A delightful way to approach the

city, and especially useful for those staying in downtown hotels (Boston Harbor, Boston Marriott Long Wharf, Bostonian, Lafayette and Hotel Meridien), is the Airport Water Shuttle (tel: 439-3131). It operates every 15 minutes Monday to Friday 6am–8pm; Saturday and Sunday every 30 minutes, on the quarter hour, from 12.15pm–7.45pm. The voyage takes 7 minutes and the fare is under $10. A free shuttle bus operates between the ferry dock and all airline terminals.

Car rentals can be arranged at the ground level of all terminals. The following firms are represented: Avis (tel: 561 3500; 1-800-331-1212); Budget (497-1800; 1-800-527-0700); Hertz (569-7272; 1-800-654-3131); National (569-6700; 1-800-227-7368).

When faced with serious traffic delays at the tunnel, take Route 1A North to Route 16 for the Tobin Bridge and then into Boston. Some useful airport telephone numbers include: Public Information Office 561-1800; Foreign Language Translators 561-1812; Traveler's Aid 542-7286.

By Rail

Boston is the northern terminus of Amtrak's Northeast Corridor ('Shore Line'). Passenger trains arrive at South Station (Atlantic Avenue and Summer Street, tel: 482-3660; 1-800-872-7245 or, for the hearing impaired, 1-800-523-6590) from New York, Washington DC, and Philadelphia, with connections from all points in the nationwide Amtrak system. They also stop at Back Bay Station (145

The river – a transport artery

Dartmouth Street, tel: 482-3660). South Station is also the eastern terminus for Amtrak's Lake Shore Limited, which travels daily between Chicago and Boston by way of Cleveland, Buffalo, Rochester and Albany.

By Bus

Several intercity bus companies serve Boston. The two largest, Greyhound and Peter Pan, have frequent daily services from New York City and Albany NY, as well as services from points within New England. Greyhound serves the entire United States and parts of Canada; its unlimited 'Ameripass' is available for 7-, 15- or 30-day periods.

Trolly traveling

Major bus terminals are Greyhound (South Station, tel: 1-800-231 2222) and Peter Pan (555 Atlantic Avenue, tel: 1-800-343-9999), across from South Station. Bonanza (tel: 720-4110, 1-800-556-3815) has its terminal at South Station. Greyhound and Peter Pan also have terminals at Riverside in Newton, on the 'D' Branch of the Green Line.

By Car

Getting to Boston: From the west: Route 90 (Mass. Pike) is the best route inbound. Three major exits: Exits 18–20, Cambridge/Allston – best for Cambridge and Charles River locations: Exit 22, Prudential Center/Copley Square – best for Back Bay, Fenway, Kenmore Square and Boston Common (via Boylston, Charles, Beacon, Park and Tremont streets): Exit 24, Expressway/downtown – best for downtown, and Route 93 access.

From the south: Routes 95, 24 and 3 all 'feed' into Route 128 East which leads to Route 93 North. Two major exits are: Kneeland Street/Chinatown – best for Back Bay, theater district and Boston Common Visitor Center (via Kneeland, Charles, Beacon, Park and Tremont streets); and Dock Square – best for Airport, North End, Waterfront and Faneuil Hall Marketplace.

From the north: Routes 95, 1 and 93 enter Boston on elevated highway structures. Four major exits: Storrow

Drive – best for Back Bay, Beacon Hill, Cambridge and Boston Common Visitor Center (via Government Center exit and Cambridge Street, which becomes Tremont Street); High Street – best for downtown; Kneeland Street – convenient for Chinatown and the theater district.

Getting Out of Boston: To the west: Take Route 90 (Mass. Pike). From downtown, enter the 'Pike' at Kneeland Street; from the Back Bay take Arlington Street, Copley Square or Mass. Avenue at Newbury Street.

To the south and the north: Route 93 (Southeast Expressway) serves the South Shore and Cape Cod (via Route 3) and Rhode Island and New York (via Routes 128 and 95). Route 93 (North) serves the North Shore and the New England Coast (via Route 1 and 95), New Hampshire (via Routes 93 and 95) and Vermont (via Routes 93 and 89).

TRAVEL ESSENTIALS
Visas & Passports

To enter the United States you must have a valid passport. Visas are required for some nationalities. Vaccinations are not required.

Customs

Anyone over 21 may take into the US 200 cigarettes, 50 cigars or 3lbs of tobacco; 1 US quart of alcohol; duty-free gifts worth up to $100. You are not permitted to bring in meat products, seeds, plants, fruits. Don't even think about bringing in narcotics. The US permits you to take out anything you wish, but consult the consulate or tourist authority of the country you are visiting next to learn of its customs regulations on entry.

Money Matters

Traveler's checks are the most convenient way to carry large sums. The two most widely accepted are American Express and Visa.
Nearly all stores, restaurants and hotels accept them, but proof of identification may be required, especially in banks. Credit cards (American Express, Visa, Mastercard, and Diners Club) are also widely honored, but be sure to double-check with waiters or clerks beforehand.

Health

Health care in the US is very expensive and foreign visitors are advised to obtain health insurance before leaving home.

What to Wear

Even more than in other parts of the country, it might be said that 'anything goes.' This is in part due to the large number of students in Boston and in part because of its international flavor. A few restaurants do demand 'jacket and tie,' however. It can be very cold in winter and very hot during summer.

Time Zones

Boston is on Eastern Standard Time. Every spring the clock is moved forward 1 hour and every fall back 1 hour. Boston is 3 hours ahead of Los Angeles, 1 hour ahead of Chicago, 5 hours behind London and 15 hours behind Tokyo.

Climate

Part of the magic of Boston is that it has four distinct seasons. The first snow generally falls in November and continues intermittently through to March. The Charles River usually freezes over. Spring, which can be fleeting, is in April and/or May. This is when magnolias and lilacs bloom and perfume fills the air. Summer months – June until September – can be very hot and humid, although for most of the time the weather is pleasantly hot – in the 70s and 80s Fahrenheit. The

Boston's ethnic mix

fall is glorious with multi-colored foliage, which peaks in mid-October as the temperature starts to plummet.

Business Hours

Most offices are open Monday to Friday 9am–5pm, although some open at 8am. Banks are open Monday to Friday 9am–3pm and often later. On Thursday some remain open until 5pm. Saturday hours are usually 9am–2pm.

The main Post Office is at 25 Dorchester Avenue, behind South Station. Post Office hours are Monday to Friday 8am–5pm; Saturday 8am–noon. The Post Office at Logan Airport remains open until midnight.

If you do not know where you will be staying, mail can be addressed to General Delivery, Main Post Office, Boston.

Information Sources

Boston Common Visitor Information Center: On the Tremont Street side of Boston Common. The booth marks the start of the Freedom Trail and provides information about Greater Boston, Massachusetts and New England. Open daily from 9am–5pm.

Faneuil Hall Marketplace Information Center (tel:248-0399): On south side of Quincy Market.

Massport International Information Booth: At Logan International Airport (Terminal E). Assistance to international visitors. Open in summer noon–8pm; in winter noon–6pm.

National Park Service Visitor Center (tel: 242-5642): At 15 State Street opposite Old State House. Open daily 9am–5pm.

Cambridge Discovery Inc. (tel: 497-1630): At booth in the center of Harvard Square. Source of comprehensive information on Cambridge. Open Monday to Saturday 9am–5pm, Sunday 11am–5pm.

Harvard University Information Office (tel: 495-1000): At Holyoke Center in Harvard Square. Source of Harvard-specific information during the academic year. Monday to Saturday 9am–4.45pm. Also on Sunday in summer 1pm–4.45pm.

Traveler's Aid Society (tel: 542-7286): At 17 East Street near South Station. Booths at Greyhound Bus Terminal and at Logan Airport, Terminals A and E.

Bostix Ticket Booth (tel: 723-5181): At Faneuil Hall and Copley Square. Boston's entertainment information center provides tickets and information for over 100 attractions. Half-price theater tickets on day of performance. Open Tuesday to Saturday 11am–6pm; Sunday 11am–4pm.

Phone Numbers

Police in Boston/Cambridge: 911
Pharmacy open 24 hours: 523-1028

(Phillips Drug, 155 Charles Street)
Medical Hot Lines: Beth Israel Hospital 735-2000
Boston Evening Medical Center 267-7171
Massachusetts General Hospital 726-2000
Disabled Information Center: 727-5540
Credit Cards Lost or Stolen: American Express 1-800-528-4800
Diners Club/Carte Blanche 1-800-525-7376
Mastercard 1-800-993-8111
Visa 1-800-847-2911
Weather: 936-1234
To dial other countries (Canada follows the US system), first dial the international access code, **011**, then the country code: **Australia** (61); **France** (33); **Germany** (49); **Italy** (39); **Japan** (81); **Mexico** (52); **Spain** (34); **United Kingdom** (44). If using a US phone credit card, dial the company's access number below, then 01, then the country code. Sprint, tel: 10333; AT&T, tel: 10288.

Tipping

Tipping is voluntary, but waiters, taxi-drivers, bartenders, and hairdressers expect 15 percent of the bill, 20 percent for above-average service. Doormen, skycabs and porters receive about $1 per bag.

MEDIA

Newspapers and Magazines

Boston Globe: Daily newspaper. Thursday supplement gives complete listings for the next seven days. *Boston Herald:* Daily newspaper. Friday supplement contains listings for the following week. *Boston Magazine*: A slick and informative monthly of local interest. *Boston Phoenix*: A thick Thursday alternative weekly with listings and comments on the local entertain-

Badge of authority

ment scene. *Where Boston*: Free glossy monthly with shoppng, dining, entertainment and attraction listings.

Out of Town News in Harvard Square (tel: 354-7777) is *the* place to purchase national and international newspapers and magazines.

Radio and Television

Radio stations in the area include: WEEI on 590AM for news; WRKO on 680AM for talk; WCRB on 102.5FM for classical music; WBCN on 104.1FM for rock music; WJIB on 96.9FM for popular music; and WGBH (Public Radio) for classical music on 89.7FM.

Some TV stations are: Channel 2 (WGBH) for public television; Channel 25 (WXNE); Channel 38 (WSBK) screens sports. National networks like CBS can be viewed on Channel 4 (WBZ); ABC on Channel 5 (WCVB) and NBC on Channel 7 (WHDH).

GETTING AROUND

Boston is a walkers' city, not a drivers' city. I advise you to park and walk. Giving the boot (wheel clamping) is a sport much favored by the police. Conveniently located, but inadequate, public parking facilities can be found at **Government Center**; **Post Office Square**; the **Prudential Center,** and elsewhere. Meters are ubiquitous, but usually occupied.

Much better by far to use the subway (aka the 'T') and bus services of the MBTA (**Massachusetts Bay Transportation Authority**). For general MBTA travel information telephone 722-3200 or 1-800-392-6100 or, for the hearing impaired, 722-5146, weekdays 6.30am–11pm, weekends 9am–6pm. For 24-hour recorded service information telephone 222-5000; for customer service telephone 722-5215; and for MBTA police emergency telephone 722-5151.

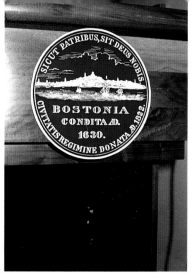

Rapid Transit

The subway, despite over-crowding at rush hours, is fairly efficient and user-friendly. The four rapid transit lines – Red, Green, Orange, Blue – that radiate out from downtown Boston still use the name 'subway' even though many of the lines run above ground for much of their route. All four lines intersect in the downtown area.

'Inbound' means toward downtown – Park Street, downtown Crossing, State Street or Government Center. 'Outbound' means away from downtown. Both the Red and Green Lines have branches that extend beyond central Boston. Check the signs on the front of the trains. Green Line trains (also called streetcars or simply cars) carry letters to indicate different branches: B–Boston College; C–Cleveland Circle; D–Riverside; E–Heath Street or Arborway. A red line through the letter on a sign means that the train goes only part way on that branch.

Turnstiles in the underground stations of the 'T' only accept tokens. These can be purchased at the collectors' booths. One token permits the traveler to ride the entire subway system, though there is a surcharge on extensions of the Green Line. When boarding the 'T' at surface stations one token or the exact change is necessary. The Rapid Transit operates 20 hours each day – from shortly after 5am until past 1am. On Sundays, services begin about 40 minutes later. The last trains leave downtown Boston at 12.45am.

MBTA bus at South Station

Buses: Only a few of MBTA's 160-plus bus routes actually enter downtown, and most of these are express services from outlying areas. One service which visitors might wish to use is Route 1, which travels along Massachusetts Avenue (at the western end of the Back Bay) across the Charles River to MIT and on to Harvard Square. Exact change is required on buses, and dollar bills are not accepted. MBTA tokens are accepted but change is not returned.

Commuter Rail

The MBTA Commuter Rail extends from downtown Boston to as far as 60 miles away and serves such tourist destinations as Concord and Salem. Trains which serve the north and the northwest of Boston depart from North Station, while trains to points south and west of the city leave from South Station. Most south side commuter trains also stop at Back Bay Station. Tickets are sold at the railway stations or can be purchased on the train, subject to a surcharge.

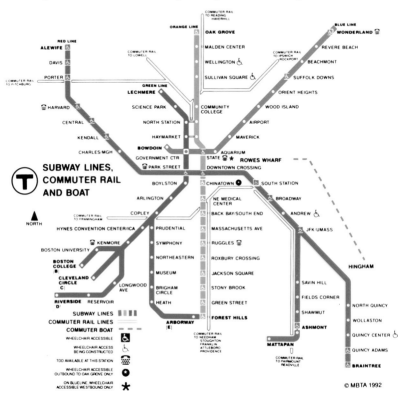

© MBTA 1992

MBTA Passport Visitor Pass

A three-day Passport costs $9; a seven-day Passport is $18. Children's Passports (age 5–11) are half the adult price. Passports permit unlimited use on the 'T', on MBTA buses up to a certain fare (additional fare, if any, payable in cash), and some commuter rail zones. Passports also produce discounts at some tourist attractions and restaurants. Passports are sold at the airport, the three railway stations, the Visitor Information Center on Boston Common, Quincy Market, the Harvard subway station and some hotels. Telephone 722-3200 for further details.

Taxicabs

A dozen taxi companies ply the streets of Boston and Cambridge, although on a rainy day you may begin to doubt that any exist at all as you wait endlessly on the sidewalk. Tolls at bridges and tunnels must be paid for by the passenger. There is no extra fare for additional passengers, but the driver may make a charge for heavy suitcases or unusual cargo. For trips over 12 miles from downtown, flat rates are charged.

Car Rental

There are numerous options and it is worth comparing prices. Companies to try include Avis (tel: 561-3500, 1-800-331-1212); Budget (tel: 497 1800, 1-800-527-0700); Dollar Rent A Car (tel: 569-5300); Hertz (tel: 338-1500, 1-800-654-3131); National (tel: 227-7368); Rent-A-Wreck (tel: 576-3700); Thrifty (tel: 569-6500, 1-800-367-2277 and Ugly Duckling Car Rental (tel: 783-3825).

Limousine Service

Contact Boston Coach, 151 Everett Avenue (Tel: 387-7676); Mini Coach of Boston (Tel: 391-1920).

Boston Harbor Hotel

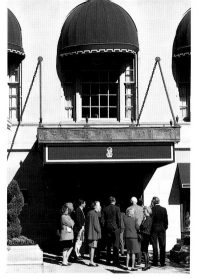

The Ritz-Carlton Hotel

ACCOMMODATIONS

Boston is reasonably endowed with hotels, although space is limited when conventions are on. The metropolitan area boasts well over 20,000 hotel rooms. Bed and breakfast accommodation is increasingly popular.

A very approximate guide to current room rates (standard double) is: $= under $100; $$=$100–150; $$$= $150–200; $$$$=over $200.

BACK BAY HILTON (335 rooms)
40 Dalton Street
Tel: 236-1100 / 1-800-874-0663
Near the Hynes Convention Center and Christian Science Complex. Close to Massachusetts Avenue and bus to Cambridge. $$$

BOSTON HARBOR HOTEL (230 rooms)
70 Rowes Wharf
Tel: 439-7000 / 1-800-752-7077
Board the Airport Water Shuttle at Logan and, minutes later, enter the

Copley Plaza Hotel

with bay windows (which open). Health club, lap-pool, sauna. $$$$

city's new signature building. All bedrooms have harbor or skyline views and all have windows that open: 18 rooms for the physically handicapped. Financial District and Quincy Market are nearby. $$$$

BOSTONIAN HOTEL (152 rooms)
Faneuil Hall Marketplace
Tel: 523-3600/1-800-343-0922
Continental elegance and intimacy. Some rooms with working fireplaces, exposed beams and brick walls. Limousine service to the airport and other parts of Boston. $$$$

COLONNADE HOTEL (280 rooms)
120 Huntington Avenue
Tel: 424-7000/1-800-962-3030
European-style hotel. Bedrooms are L-shaped with distinct sitting, sleeping and dressing areas. Well situated close to the Prudential Center, with subway stop at the doorstep. Seasonal rooftop pool. $$$

COPLEY PLAZA HOTEL (393 rooms)
138 St James Avenue
Tel: 267-5300/1-800-225-7654
Grande dame of Boston hotels, with a European style. Situated in Copley Square, close to most tourist attractions. Subway at the doorstep. $$$$

FOUR SEASONS HOTEL (288 rooms)
200 Boylston Street
Tel: 338-4400/1-800-332-3442
Elegant red-brick hotel overlooking the Public Garden. Large bedrooms

LENOX HOTEL (220 rooms)
710 Boylston Street
Tel: 536-5300/1-800-225-7676
Traditional family hotel built in 1900. Some bedrooms have functional fireplaces. A few steps from the Prudential Center and Copley Place. $$

LE MERIDIEN (326 rooms)
250 Franklin Street
Tel: 451-1900/543-4300
Formerly the Federal Reserve Bank, which in turn was modelled on a Roman palazzo. Close to Quincy Market. Pool and health club. $$$$

OMNI PARKER HOUSE (541 rooms)
60 School Street
Tel: 227-8600/1-800-843-6664
Possibly the most centrally located hotel in the city Claims to be the oldest continually operating hotel in America $$$

RITZ-CARLTON HOTEL (278 rooms)
15 Arlington Street
Tel: 536-5700/1-800-241-3333
The nation's first Ritz and still the city's *numero uno* with the highest staff-to-guest ratio in town. View of Public Garden. The Back Bay on the doorstep. Limousine service within city on weekday mornings. $$$$

SHERATON BOSTON HOTEL & TOWERS (1,2500 rooms)
39 Dalton Street
Tel: 236-2000/1-800-325-3535
New England's largest hotel, near the Prudential Center. $$$$

SWISSOTEL BOSTON (500 rooms)
1 Avenue de Lafayette
Tel: 451-2600/1-800-621-9200
Grand, elegant hotel in the heart of downtown. $$$$

Tremont House (281 rooms)
275 Tremont Street
Tel: 426-1400/1-800-331-9998
In the theater district, close to most
tourist attractions. **$$**

Westin Hotel (804 rooms)
Copley Place
Tel: 262-9600/1-800-228-3000
Boston's tallest hotel; 40 rooms for
the physically handicapped. Pool and
health club. **$$$$**

In Cambridge

The Charles Hotel (299 rooms)
1 Bennett Street
Tel: 864-1200/1-800-882-1818
On the edge of Harvard Square. Shop-
ping mall and restaurants all around.
Health club. **$$**

Inn at Harvard
(113 rooms)
1201 Massachusetts Avenue
Tel: 491-2222/1-800-458-5886
A stylish new inn which can be found
at Harvard's gates. **$$**

Commander (176 rooms)
16 Garden Street
Tel: 547-4800, 1-800-528-0444
Near Harvard Yard Some rooms have
kitchenettes; some have Boston rock-
ers and four-posters. **$$$**

Bed&Breakfast/Guest Houses

A room usually costs about $100
for two persons.

Baileys/Boston House
(10 rooms)
331 Beacon Street
Tel: 262-4543
European-style B&B in the Back
Bay.

Beacon Hill Bed & Breakfast
27 Brimmer Street
Tel: 523-7376

All rooms with fireplace, double or
queen-size bed and private bath. Smok-
ing not permitted.

Bed & Breakfast Agency of Boston
47 Commercial Wharf
Tel: 720-3540
Offers turn-of-the-century townhouses
and furnished condos.

Host Homes of Boston
P.O Box 117, Newton, MA02168
Tel 244-1308
A moored yacht in the harbor and a
Victorian townhouse in the Back Bay
are just some of the unusual listings.

Newbury Guest House
216 Newbury Street
Tel: 437-7666
This is a friendly guest house in the
heart of the Back Bay.

FURTHER READING

Insight Guide: Boston, edited by Marcus Brooke, Apa Publications. Com-
bines detailed and insightful reporting
about what makes Boston tick with
a daring photo-journalistic style of il-
lustration.
Insight Guide: New England, edited
by Jay Itzkowitz, Apa Publications.
In-depth coverage of the whole of New
England.

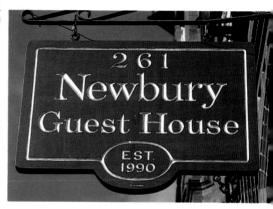

B&B in Back Bay

Index

ACKNOWLEDGMENTS

Photography	Marcus Brooke *and*
pages 2/3	Steve Dunwell
65	Gene Peach
Production Editor	Mohammed Dar
Handwriting	V Barl
Cover Design	Klaus Geisler
Cartography	Berndtson & Berndtson